HISTORY NOTES

Daniel L. Fountain

Meredith College
Raleigh, North Carolina

OUT OF MANY
A HISTORY
OF THE AMERICAN PEOPLE
VOLUME I

SIXTH EDITION

John Mack Faragher
Yale University

Mary Jo Buhle
Brown University

Daniel Czitrom
Mt. Holyoke College

Susan H. Armitage
Washington State University

PEARSON

Prentice
Hall

Upper Saddle River, New Jersey 074⌐⌐

D1361475

© 2009 by PEARSON EDUCATION, INC.
Upper Saddle River, New Jersey 07458

All rights reserved

10 9 8 7 6 5 4 3 2 1

ISBN 10: 0-13-602836-5
ISBN 13: 978-0-13-602836-9

Printed in the United States of America

TABLE OF CONTENTS

1. A CONTINENT OF VILLAGES, TO 1500

CHAPTER OVERVIEW

Summary

The Indians of North, Central and South America comprised a highly diverse and successful set of civilizations prior to the arrival of Columbus in the late fifteenth century. On the North American continent this diversity is evidenced by the cultures which developed in deserts of the southwest, the grasslands of the Great Plains, and the forested regions east of the Mississippi. While many Indian peoples were mobile and powerful hunters who used innovations like the Clovis point to improve their acquisition of game, they could also be highly successful farmers whose agricultural prowess allowed them to develop and maintain significant urban populations. Throughout the period before Columbus, these diverse peoples engaged in long distance trade with, waged war against, and in some cases allied with their neighboring tribes in what was a dynamic, developed living environment. Clearly, Columbus did not discover a "new" world, but instead became among the first people to introduce old and well-established traditions to one another.

Focus Questions

1. How were the Americas first settled?

2. In what ways did native communities adapt to the distinct regions of North America?

3. What were the consequences of the development of farming for native communities?

4. What was the nature of the Indian cultures in the three regions where Europeans first invaded and settled?

CHAPTER REVIEW

Short Response: Consider these questions thoughtfully. Respond with the best possible short answer by filling in the blank.

1. The large powerful city state that existed along the Mississippi River during the thirteenth century was
    _____.

2. When Columbus landed in the New World, he mistakenly used the Spanish word _____ to identify the native inhabitants.

3. Genetic evidence strongly suggests that the Indian people migrated to North America from
    _____.

4. The sophisticated fluted blades that were a major innovation in hunting were known as
    _____ points.

5. The warming of the Earth that led to the end of the Ice Age occurred approximately _____ years ago.

6. In the Penobscot legend about the origin of native food traditions, the _____ sacrifices herself for the good of the Indian people.

7. In the lands east of the Mississippi River, a sophisticated knowledge of the region's diverse plant and animal life allowed the Indian tribes of that region to enjoy what anthropologists describe as _____.

8. The Indian civilization of the Yucatan Peninsula who possessed a sophisticated knowledge of calendar systems and mathematics was the _____.

9. The bow and arrow was first developed in the _____ before eventually spreading to other areas of North America.

10. Several northeastern tribes, which occupied contemporary Ontario and upstate New York, banded together to form the _____ under the leadership of Chief Deganawida.

Multiple Choice: Select the response that best answers each question or best completes each sentence.

1. The massive earthworks of the lost city of Cahokia are located nearest to which modern city of the Mississippi River Valley?
   a. Memphis, TN.
   b. St. Louis, MO.
   c. Jackson, MS.
   d. Minneapolis, MN.

2. Beringia is best described as:
   a. a major Indian settlement of the Eastern Woodlands.
   b. one of the principal migration paths used by Asian peoples who migrated to North America.
   c. an early leader of the Athapascan peoples.
   d. an important technological development of ancient Americans.

3. The Clovis tradition:
   a. was a construction technique that enabled Indian Peoples to build structures high upon cliffs.
   b. refers to the Zuni account of creation.
   c. was a powerful new technology that enabled Indian peoples to be more successful hunters.
   d. is an archaeological theory of how ancient Americans first used horses to hunt bison.

4. Recent archeological evidence has led some scholars to conclude that early migration in North America:
   a. relied on dog sleds to carry people over the vast glacial sheets that covered the continent.
   b. occurred by water as people used boats to travel along the western coastline of the continent.
   c. could not have taken place as long as the continent was covered by the vast glaciers of the Ice Age.
   d. took place as human beings sought fertile lands to ensure the production of abundant food crops.

5. The retreat of the glaciers during the Archaic Period led to all of the following new ways of finding food except:
   a. hunting in the artic.
   b. foraging in the arid deserts.
   c. hunting and gathering in the forests.
   d. farming of drought tolerant wheat in the desert.

6. Farming radically changed the social environment of Indian peoples in which of the following ways:
   a. reducing the amount of land needed to support existing populations.

b. led to the appearance of villages and permanent architecture.

c. more organized methods of the storage and distribution of food.

d. All of the Above.

7. The "miracle crops" that first emerged in North America were:
   a. wheat and rice.
   b. maize and potatoes.
   c. beans and squash.
   d. barley and rye.

8. When using the term "resisted revolution," historians are referring to:
   a. the refusal of some Indian groups to shift to an agricultural society.
   b. Indians' effort to prevent Europeans from creating colonies in North America.
   c. the southwestern tribes' practice of refusing to trade with Europeans.
   d. an uprising at Cahokia that the power elite brutally suppressed.

9. Large, densely settled Indian communities first developed in:
   a. Mesoamerica.
   b. the Mississippi River Valley.
   c. the Great Basin.
   d. the Eastern Woodlands.

10. The Anasazis were:
    a. responsible for the founding the great city of Teotihuacan.
    b. a farming and cliff dwelling culture group of the Four Corners Area.
    c. the "ancient enemies" of the Eastern Woodland warriors.
    d. driven from their ancestral lands by uncontrollable flooding.

11. The practice of mound building is mostly associated with:
    a. the Woodland Peoples of the Ohio Valley.
    b. early methods of flood control along the upper reaches of the Missouri River.
    c. defensive strategies related to the development of Clovis points.
    d. innovative farming techniques of the forest dwelling Anasazi peoples.

12. All of the following describe warfare and violence among Indian peoples except:
    a. extended drought may have greatly increased violence and social disorder.
    b. organized violence was probably rare among hunting bands.
    c. warfare was nonexistent among farming confederacies before Europeans arrived.
    d. the first Europeans to arrive in the Southeast described highly organized combat among large tribal armies.

13. Before the colonial era, Indian peoples:
    a. were primarily nomadic hunter-gatherer societies.
    b. developed diverse societies which were adapted to the regional environment.
    c. primarily lived in complex, highly urban communities like Cahokia.
    d. lived in regionally isolated enclaves that had little to no contact with other tribes.

14. The Iroquois Confederacy:
    a. attempted to control social violence by prohibiting warfare among member nations.
    b. constituted the most important of the Indian alliances in the western United States.
    c. included the Algonquin Indians, who were the largest tribe in North America.
    d. remained a hunting and gathering society until Europeans introduced livestock.

15. The Natchez are an example:
    a. of a peaceful, egalitarian Indian society that existed before colonization.
    b. of a hierarchical society that celebrated warriors and practiced human sacrifice.
    c. of an Indian society that historians know virtually nothing about.
    d. was the first tribe to make contact with Columbus.

Thought Questions: Think carefully about the following questions or comments. Your answers should prepare you to participate in class discussions or help you to write an effective essay. In both class discussions and essays you should always support the arguments you make by referring to specific examples and historical evidence. You may use the space provided to sketch out ideas or outline your response.

1. Describe the early North American Indian societies that were based on the hunting tradition, the Desert Culture, or the forest efficiency. In what regions of North America were these traditions most prevalent?

2. How did the emergence of agriculture shape the lives and cultures of American Indians?

3. Why did some Indian groups resist the transition toward agricultural societies and economies?

4. What are the distinctive "cultural areas" of North America that existed on the eve of colonization? What were the major characteristics of these cultural areas and what were the principal factors that led them to develop in that manner?

Map Skills: These questions are based on the maps in the chapter. Please use the blank map provided here for your answers.

1. Locate Beringia and the major migration routes into North America.

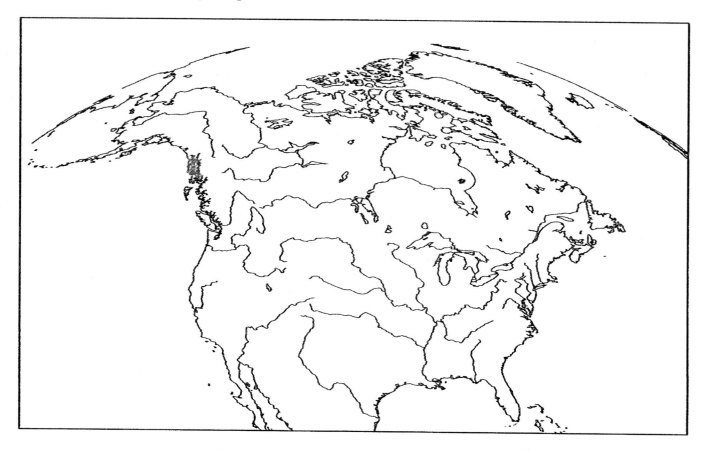

2. Identify the major areas of Indian settlement prior to the arrival of Europeans.

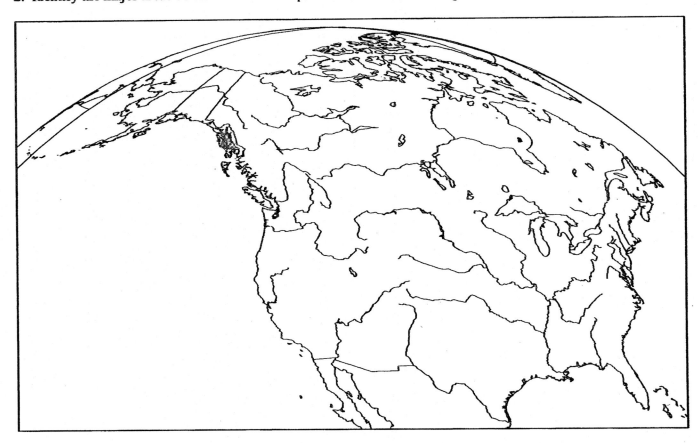

3. What are some examples of how geography shaped the lives and cultures of Indian peoples? Use the map above to identify regions that left a distinctive imprint on the Indian peoples who settled there.

Interpreting the Past

Name _____ **Date** _____

Defend or refute the following statement: Native American peoples that European explorers encountered in North America prior to 1500 were highly civilized and coordinated tribes.

DOCUMENT 1

DOCUMENT 2

DOCUMENT 3

DOCUMENT 4

DOCUMENT 5

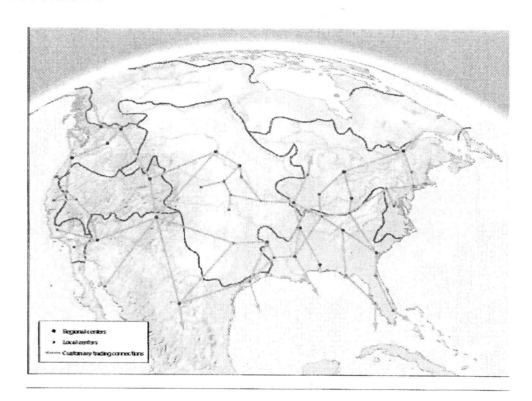

DOCUMENT 6

DOCUMENT 7

DOCUMENT 8

DOCUMENT 9

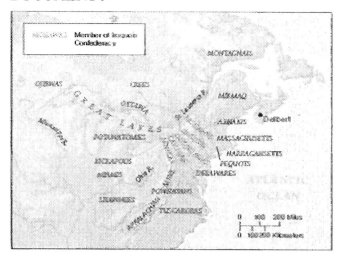

DOCUMENT 10

Source: Thomas Harriot (1560–1621)

They are a people clothes with loffe mantles made of Deere skins, & aprons of the same rounde about their middles; all els naked; of such a difference of statures only as wee in England; having no edge tooles or wewapons of yron or steele to offend us…by the experience we have had in some places, the turning up of the heels against us in running away was their best defence.

2. WHEN WORLDS COLLIDE, 1492–1590

CHAPTER OVERVIEW

Summary

The arrival of the Spanish in the Western Hemisphere triggered a period of dramatic global change. Columbus and the conquistadors who followed him helped spur a transfer of flora and fauna between the Old and New Worlds. The resulting Columbian Exchange led to enormous cultural and economic developments throughout the world as goods like tobacco, corn, and sugar entered into the global marketplace. While the world has benefited from many aspects of this exchange, the Indian peoples of the Western Hemisphere paid a terrible price for this global transfer. Indian populations who had no immunity to Old World diseases saw their populations melt under a literal torrent of epidemics. The remaining Indian peoples thus faced ambitious European warriors and colonists in a greatly weakened state which left many vulnerable to conquest. As news of Spanish colonial success and subsequent wealth reached Europe, other nations were eager to join in the process of exploration and colonization.

Focus Questions

1. What was the European background to the colonization of North America?

2. What kind of an empire did the Spanish create in the New World, and why did it extend into North America?

3. In what ways did the exchange of peoples, crops, animals, and diseases shape the experience of European colonists and American natives?

4. What was the French role in the beginning of the North American fur trade?

5. Why did England enter the race for colonies?

CHAPTER REVIEW

Short Response: Consider these questions thoughtfully. Respond with the best possible short answer by filling in the blank.

1. The first English child born in the New World was _____.

2. The English settlement on Roanoke Island was sponsored by _____.

3. _____ was the European social system in which land was divided into hundreds of small territories, each of which was ruled by a family of lords who possessed a monopoly of power.

4. The _____ was an intellectual movement which helped fuel European curiosity about the world around them.

5. _____ was the first Portuguese explorer to reach India.

6. The institution in which Indian peoples were obliged to work for Spanish lords in the New World was known as the _____.

7. The author of the sixteenth century work *The Destruction of the Indies* was _____.

8. _____ was the first conquistador to attempt to extend the Spanish Empire into North America.

9. The _____ was the legal device which attempted to divide the Western Hemisphere between Portugal and Spain.

10. The German priest who triggered the Protestant Reformation was _____.

Multiple Choice: Select the response that best answers each question or best completes each sentence.

1. The English colony established on Roanoke Island in 1587:
   a. defeated and replaced an earlier built Spanish trading post.
   b. mysteriously disappeared within a few years of being established.
   c. eventually surrendered to Spanish military forces in 1595.
   d. succeeded only after moving inland to find a healthier climate.

2. All of the following were features of European life before 1500 except:
   a. a majority of the population was peasant farmers.
   b. feudalism was the dominant social system.
   c. famine and disease periodically ravaged the land.
   d. deep religious divisions between Protestants and Catholics.

3. The European commercialism that characterized the Renaissance was fueled in part by:
   a. the emergence of English city states that traded with Muslim merchants of the Mediterranean.
   b. the support that the agricultural lower classes provided to the powerful urban bourgeois class.
   c. the sharp decline in the population of the merchant class that occurred in the years after 1500.
   d. the close relationships between the emerging national monarchs and the developing merchant class.

4. During the mid to late 1400s the Portuguese:
   a. opposed trade with Sub-Saharan Africa because it benefited its Muslim rivals.
   b. were leaders in both adopting seafaring innovations and Atlantic Ocean exploration.
   c. lost out to their Spanish commercial rivals because their leaders believed the world was flat.
   d. captured Constantinople and gained a monopoly on the Asian spice trade.

5. In 1492 the struggle to expel Muslim invaders from the Iberian Peninsula came to an end. This conflict is known as the:
    a. Crusades.
    b. Spanish Inquisition.
    c. Reconquista.
    d. Armada.

6. Which of the following was not a major factor in the Spanish decision to support Columbus's expedition?
    a. concern over Portugal's successful exploration of the West African Coast.
    b. a long-standing tradition of military conquest.
    c. the prospect of international trade.
    d. rumors of an English colony in the Western Atlantic.

7. During Columbus's first voyage he:
    a. explored several islands of the Caribbean including some of the Bahamas, Cuba, and Hispaniola.
    b. landed in Florida and claimed it for Spain.
    c. realized that he had discovered new continents.
    d. became convinced that the native inhabitants were too barbaric to convert to Christianity.

8. The Western Hemisphere was first described as Mundus Novus, a "New World" by:
    a. Christopher Columbus.
    b. Vasco da Gama.
    c. Prince Henry the Navigator.
    d. Amerigo Vespucci.

9. Critical to the success of the Hernán Cortés expedition:
    a. were Indian allies and European disease.
    b. were the French fleet and the Spanish army.
    c. was the overwhelming number of Spaniards.
    d. was the Aztec rebellion against Montezuma.

10. As a result of the Columbian Exchange that occurred after 1492, three important crops transplanted to the New World were:
    a. chocolate, corn, and tobacco.
    b. apples, potatoes, and wheat.
    c. coffee, rice, and sugarcane.
    d. cloves, nutmeg, and pepper.

11. Bartolome de las Casas and Antonio de Montesinos were:
    a. the principal commanders in the conquest of the Aztecs and Inca.
    b. Catholic clergymen who protested Spanish mistreatment of the Indians.
    c. the first Europeans to land in Brazil.
    d. criticized by world leaders for ignoring the Pope's command to convert the Indians.

12. The oldest continuously occupied European city in North America is:
    a. Jamestown, VA.
    b. Plymouth, MA.
    c. Boston, MA.
    d. St. Augustine, FL.

13. The early French efforts in America were based on commerce, especially the trade in:
    a. forest products.
    b. gold and silver.

    c. animal furs.
    d. food stuffs.

14. An important element in encouraging the English interest in the New World was:
    a. England's military alliance with the French.
    b. economic dislocations throughout England.
    c. England's desire to spread Catholicism.
    d. territory gained by her through the Treaty of Tordesillas.

15. In 1517, what major religious event began which later influenced European decisions to colonize North America?
    a. Henry VIII of England founded the Church of England.
    b. The Spanish Inquisition drove Muslims and Jews from Spain.
    c. Martin Luther triggered the Protestant Reformation by criticizing the Roman Catholic Church.
    d. French Huguenots attempted to create a colony in Florida.

Thought Questions: Think carefully about the following questions or comments. Your answers should prepare you to participate in class discussions or help you to write an effective essay. In both class discussions and essays you should always support the arguments you make by referring to specific examples and historical evidence. You may use the space provided to sketch out ideas or outline your response.

1. Describe the social, economic, and political changes that occurred in Europe after 1300 that led to the era of exploration and expansion. What were the most important developments or ideas that contributed to these changes?

2. What role did diseases play in Europe and in America during the years 1492 to 1590? What impact did disease have on European colonization efforts that took place during this period?

3. Describe the Columbian exchange that took place after 1492 and discuss the implications that resulted from the collision of the Old and New Worlds. In particular, how is the world different today as a result of this exchange?

4. How and why did the Protestant Reformation influence European expansion into the Americas?

Map Skills: These questions are based on the maps in the chapter. Please use the blank map provided here for your answers.

1. Locate the following places: Azores Islands, Madeira Islands, Portugal, Spain, France, and England. How did geography help nations like Portugal, Spain, France, and England lead the way in Atlantic exploration?

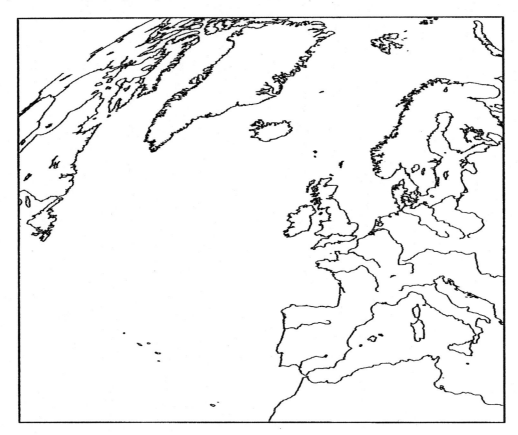

2. Identify the areas of early North American exploration by the Spanish, the French, the English, the Dutch, and the Swedes. What factors influenced these European nations to target the areas they explored or attempted to settle?

Interpreting the Past

Name _____ Date _____

Defend or refute the following statement: The colonization of North America was primarily a religious endeavor.

DOCUMENT 1

Christopher Columbus, Letter to Ferdinand and Isabella of Spain (1494)
Source: AmDocs Website, University of Kansas, http://www.ukans.edu/carrie/docs/texts/columlet.html

1. That in the said island there shall be founded three or four towns, situated in the most convenient places, and that the settlers who are there be assigned to the aforesaid places and towns.
2. That for the better and more speedy colonization of the said island, no one shall have liberty to collect gold in it except those who have taken out colonists' papers, and have built houses for their abode, in the town in which they are, that they may live united and in greater safety.
3. That each town shall have its alcalde [Mayor] . . . and its notary public, as is the use and custom in Castile.
4. That there shall be a church, and parish priests or friars to administer the sacraments, to perform divine worship, and for the conversion of the Indians.
5. That none of the colonists shall go to seek gold without a license from the governor or alcalde of the town where he lives; and that he must first take oath to return to the place whence he sets out, for the purpose of registering faithfully all the gold he may have found, and to return once a month, or once a week, as the time may have been set for him, to render account and show the quantity of said gold; and that this shall be written down by the notary before the alcalde, or, if it seems better, that a friar or priest, deputed for the purpose, shall be also present.
6. That all the gold thus brought in shall be smelted immediately, and stamped with some mark that shall distinguish each town; and that the portion which belongs to your Highnesses shall be weighed, and given and consigned to each alcalde in his own town, and registered by the above-mentioned priest or friar, so that it shall not pass through the hands of only one person, and there shall be no opportunity to conceal the truth.
7. That all gold that may be found without the mark of one of the said towns in the possession of any one who has once registered in accordance with the above order shall be taken as forfeited, and that the accuser shall have one portion of it and your Highnesses the other.
8. That one per centum of all the gold that may be found shall be set aside for building churches and adorning the same, and for the support of the priests or friars belonging to them; and, if it should be thought proper to pay any thing to the alcaldes or notaries for their services, or for ensuring the faithful perforce of their duties, that this amount shall be sent to the governor or treasurer who may be appointed there by your Highnesses.

DOCUMENT 2

Jacques Cartier: First Contact with the Indians (1534)
Source: "The First Relation of Jacques Cartier of S. Malo," in Henry S. Burrage, ed., Early English and French Voyages, Chiefly from Hakluyt, Original Narratives of Early American History (New York: Charles Scribner's Sons, 1906).

How our men set up a great Crosse upon the poynt of the sayd Porte, and the Captaine of those wild men, after a long Oration, was by our Captain appeased, and contented that two of his Children should goe with him. Upon the 25 of the moneth, wee caused a faire high Crosse to be made of the height of thirty foote, which was made in the presence of many of them, upon the point of the entrance of the sayd haven, (6) in the middest whereof we hanged up a Shield with three Floure de Luces in it, and in the top was carved in the wood with Anticke letters this posie, Vive le Roy de France. Then before them all we set it upon the sayd point. They with great heed beheld both the making and setting of it up So soone as it was up, we altogether kneeled downe before them, with our hands toward Heaven, yeelding God thankes: and we made signes unto them, shewing them the Heavens, and that all our salvation dependeth onely on him which in them dwelleth: whereat they shewed a great admiration, looking first one at another, and then upon the Crosse. And after wee were returned to our ships, their Captaine clad with an old Beares skin, with three of his sonnes, and a brother of his with him, came unto us in one of their boates, but they came not so neere us as they were wont to doe: there he made a long Oration unto us, shewing us the crosse we had set up, and making a crosse with two fingers, then did he shew us all the Countrey about us, as if he would say that all was his, and that wee should not set up any crosse without his leave.

DOCUMENT 3

Reasons for the Plantation in New England (1629)
Source: The Winthrop Society, 1996–2001, http://www.winthropsociety.org/document.htm

Reasons to be considered for justifying the undertakers of the intended Plantation in New England, and for encouraging such whose hearts God shall move to join with them in it.
1. It will be a service to the Church of great consequence to carry the Gospel into those parts of the world, to help on the fullness of the coming of the Gentiles, and to raise a bulwark against the kingdom of AnteChrist, which the Jesuits labor to rear up in those parts.
2. All other Churches of Europe are brought to desolation, and our sins, for which the Lord begins already to frown upon us and to cut us short, do threaten evil times to be coming upon us, and who knows, but that God hath provided this place to be a refuge for many whom he means to save out of the general calamity, and seeing the Church hath no place left to fly into but the wilderness, what better work can there be, than to go and provide tabernacles and food for her when she be restored.
3. This England grows weary of her inhabitants, so as Man, who is the most precious of all creatures, is here more vile and base than the earth we tread upon, and of less price among us than a horse or a sheep. Masters are forced by authority to entertain servants, parents to maintain their own children, all towns complain of their burden to maintain their poor, though we have taken up many unnecessary, yea unlawful, trades to maintain them. We use the authority of the Law to hinder the increase of our people, as by urging the statute against cottages and inmates—and thus it is come to pass, that children, servants and neighbors, especially if they be poor, are counted the greatest burdens, which if things were right would be the chiefest earthly blessings.
4. The whole earth is the Lord's garden, and He hath given it to mankind with a general commission (Gen. 1:28) to increase and multiply and replenish the earth and subdue it, which was again renewed to Noah. The end is double and natural, that Mankind might enjoy the fruits of the earth, and God might have His due Glory from His creatures. Why then should one strive here for places of habitation, at such a cost as would obtain better land in another country, and at the same time suffer a whole continent as fruitful and convenient for the use of man to lie waste without any improvement?
5. We are grown to that height of intemperance in all excess of riot that as no man's estate, almost, will suffice to keep sail with his equals. He who fails herein must live in scorn and contempt. Hence it comes that all arts and trades are carried on in that deceitful and unrighteous course, so that it is almost impossible for a good and upright man to maintain his charge and live comfortably in any of them.
6. The fountains of learning and religion are so corrupted that most children (besides the unsupportable charge of their education) are perverted, corrupted, and utterly overthrown by the multitude of evil examples and the licentious government of those seminaries, where men strain at gnats and swallow camels, and use all severity for maintenance of caps and like accomplishments, but suffer all ruffianlike fashions and disorder in manners to pass uncontrolled.
7. What can be a better work, and more honorable and worthy of a Christian than to help rise and support a particular church while it is in its infancy, and to join his forces with such a company of faithful people, as by a timely assistance may grow strong and prosper, when for want of such help may be put to great hazard, if not wholly ruined.

DOCUMENT 4

DOCUMENT 5

The Trial of Anne Hutchinson (1638)
Source: The American Colonist's Library, Primary Source Documents Pertaining to Early American History,
http://personal.pitnet.net/primarysources/hutchinson.html

MR. NOWEL [ASSISTANT TO THE COURT]: How do you know that was the spirit?

MRS. H.: How did Abraham know that it was God that bid him offer his son, being a breach of the sixth commandment?

DEP. GOV.: By an immediate voice.

MRS. H.: So to me by an immediate revelation.

DEP. GOV.: How! an immediate revelation.

MRS. H.: By the voice of his own spirit to my soul. I will give you another scripture, Jer[emiah] 46: 27–28—out of which the Lord showed me what he would do for me and the rest of his servants. But after he was pleased to reveal himself to me I did presently, like Abraham, run to Hagar. And after that he did let me see the atheism of my own heart, for which I begged of the Lord that it might not remain in my heart, and being thus, he did show me this (a twelvemonth after) which I told you of before.. . . Therefore, I desire you to look to it, for you see this scripture fulfilledthis day and therefore I desire you as you tender the Lord and the church and commonwealth to consider and look what you do. You have power over my body but the Lord Jesus hath power over my body and soul; and assure yourselves thus much, you do as much as in you lies to put the Lord Jesus Christ from you, and if you go on in this course you begin, you will bring a curse upon you and your posterity, and the mouth of the Lord hath spoken it.

DEP. GOV.: What is the scripture she brings?

MR. STOUGHTON [ASSISTANT TO THE COURT]: Behold I turn away from you.

MRS. H.: But now having seen him which is invisible I fear not what man can do unto me.

GOV.: Daniel was delivered by miracle; do you think to be deliver'd so too?

MRS. H.: I do here speak it before the court. I look that the Lord kshould deliver me by his providence... [because God had said to her] though I should meet with affliction, yet I am the same God that delivered Daniel out of the lion's den, I will also deliver thee.

MR. HARLAKENDEN [ASSISTANT TO THE COURT]: I may read scripture and the most glorious hypocrite may read them and yet go down to hell.

MRS. H.: It may be so.. . .

GOV.: I am persuaded that the revelation she brings forth is delusion.

[The trial text here reads:] All the court but some two or three ministers cry out, we all believe it—we all believe it. [Mrs. Hutchinson was found guilty]

DOCUMENT 6

A Jesuit Priest Describes New Amsterdam (1642)
Source: New Netherlands in 1644, by Rev. Isaac Jogues, S.J. http://www.lihistory.com/

The river, which is very straight and runs due north and south, is at least a league broad before the fort. Ships lie at anchor in a bay which forms the other side of the island and can be defended from the fort. Shortly before I arrived there three large vessels of 300 tons each had come to load wheat; two had found cargoes, the third could not be loaded because the savages had burnt a part of their grain. These ships came from the West Indies where the West India Company usually keeps up seventeen ships of war. No religion is publicly exercised but the Calvinist, and orders are to admit none but Calvinists, but this is not observed, for there are, besides Calvinists, in the Colony Catholics, English Puritans, Lutherans, Anabaptists, here called Muistes &c.When any one comes to settle in the country, they lend him horses, cows &c, they give him provisions, all which he repays as soon as he is at ease, and as to the land he pays in to the West India Company after ten years the tenth of the produce which he reaps. This country is bounded on the New England side by a river they call the Fresche river, which serves as a boundary between them and the English. The English however come very near to them preferring to hold lands under the Dutch who ask nothing from them rather than to be dependent on English Lords who exact rents and would fain be absolute. On the other side southward towards Virginia, its limits are the river which they call the South river on which there is also a Dutch settlement, but the Swedes have at its mouth another extremely well provided with men and cannon. It is believed that these Swedes are maintained by some merchants of Amsterdam, who are not satisfied that the West India Company should alone enjoy all the commerce of these parts. It is near this river that a gold mine is reported to have been found.

DOCUMENT 7

George Alsop, The Importance of Tobacco (1660)
Source: George Alsop, A Character of the Province of Maryland (Baltimore: Maryland Historical Society Fund, Publication No. 15, 1880), pp. 475–477

The three main Commodities this Country affords for Trafique, are Tobacco, Furrs, and Flesh. Furrs and Skins, as Beavers, Otters, Musk-Rats, Rackoons, Wild-Cats, and Elke or Buffeloe, with divers others, which were first made vendible by the Indians of the Country, and sold to the Inhabitant, and by them to the Merchant, and so transported into England and other places where it becomes most commodious.

Tobacco is the only solid Staple Commodity of this Province: The use of it was first found out by the Indians many Ages agoe, and transferr'd into Christendom by that great Discoverer of America Columbus. It's generally made byall the Inhabitants of this Province, and between the months of March and April they sow the seed (which is much smaller then Mustard-seed) in small beds and patches digg'd up and made so by art, and about May the Plants commonly appear green in those beds: In June they are transplanted from their beds, and set in little hillocks in distant rowes, dug up for the same purpose; some twice or thrice they are weeded, and succoured from their illegitimate Leaves that would be peeping out from the body of the Stalk. They top the several Plants, as they find occasion in their predominating rankness: About the middle of September they cut the Tobacco down, and carry it into houses, (made for that purpose) to bring it to its purity: And after it has attained, by a convenient attendance upon time, to its perfection, it is then tyed up in bundles, and packt into Hogs-heads, and then laid by for the Trade. Between November and January there arrives in this Province Shipping to the number of twenty sail and upwards, all Merchant-men loaden with Commodities to Trafique and dispose of, trucking with the Planter for Silks, Hollands, Serges, and Broad-clothes, with other necessary Goods, priz'd at such and such rates as shall be judg'd on is fair and legal, for Tobacco at so much the pound, and advantage on both sides considered; the Planter for his work, and the Merchant for adventuring himself and his Commodity into so far a Country: Thus is the Trade on both sides drove on with a fair and honest Decorum. The Inhabitants of this Province are seldom or never put to the affrightment of being robb'd of their money, nor to dirty their Fingers by telling of vast sums: They have more bags to carry Corn, then Coyn; and though they want, but why should I call that a want which is only a necessary miss? the very effects of the dirt of this Province affords as great a profit to the general Inhabitant, as the Gold of Peru doth to the straight-breecht Commonalty of the Spaniard. Our Shops and Exchanges of Mary-Land, are the Merchants Store-houses, where with few words and protestations Goods are bought and delivered; not like those Shop-keepers Boys in London, that continually cry, What do ye lack Sir? What d'ye buy? yelping with so wide a mouth, as if some Apothecary had hired their mouths to stand open to catch Gnats and Vagabond Flyes in.

Tobacco is the currant Coyn of Mary-Land, and will sooner purchase Commodities from the Merchant, then money. I must confess the New-England men that trade into this Province, had rather have fat Pork for their Goods, than Tobacco or Furrs, which I conceive is, because their bodies being fast bound up with the cords of restringent Zeal, they are fain to make use of the lineaments of this Non-Canaanite creature physically to loosen them; for a bit of a pound upon a two-peny Rye loaf, according to the original Receipt, will bring the cos tiv'st red-ear'd Zealot in some three hours time to a fine stool, if methodically observed. Medera-Wines, Sugars, Salt, Wickar-Chairs, and Tin Candlesticks, is the most of the Commodities they bring in They arrive in Mary-Land about September, being most of them Ketches and Barkes, and such Small Vessels, and these dispersing themselves into several small Creeks of this Province, to sell and dispose of their Commodities, where they know the Market is most fit for their small Adventures. ...

3. PLANTING COLONIES IN NORTH AMERICA, 1588–1701

CHAPTER OVERVIEW

Summary

Before 1600, North America was subject to only limited exploration and even more limited settlement. During the seventeenth century this pattern would end as nations like England, France, and the Netherlands sought to join Spain in gaining both a foothold and wealth in the New World. Employing either a frontier of exclusion or inclusion, these European powers began to carve out new colonies in places like Chesapeake Bay, the Hudson River Valley, and along the St. Lawrence River. Wherever these aspiring colonial powers made their presence felt, they encountered a native population who was forced to come to grips with new opportunities, challenges, and realities. In some cases, as in the Pueblo Revolt and King Philip's War, Indian peoples waged war to protect their homes and ways of life.

Focus Questions

1. In what ways were the Spanish, French, and English colonies in North America similar? In what ways were they different?

2. What was the nature of the colonial encounter between English newcomers and Algonquian natives in the Chesapeake?

3. How did religious dissent shape the history of the New England colonies?

4. What role did the restored Stuart monarchy play in the creation of new proprietary colonies?

5. Why did warfare and internal conflict characterize the late seventeenth century?

CHAPTER REVIEW

Short Response: Consider these questions thoughtfully. Respond with the best possible short answer by filling in the blank.

1. The Pueblo Revolt of 1680 took place in the Spanish mission of _____.

2. According to the authors, in establishing its colonies in the New World, the English established frontiers of
    _____.

3. _____ are persons of mixed Indian and European ancestry.

4. The thousands of French "hired men" who journeyed to New France were called _____.

5. The Dutch colony on Manhattan Island was called _____.

6. The Indian peoples that early settlers at Jamestown encountered were members of the
    _____ Confederacy.

7. The Jamestown colony managed to survive two major wars that the Powhatan Confederacy fought against
    them under the leadership of Chief _____.

8. The Plymouth colonists sailed for the New World on the _____.

9. The author of the *History of Plimouth Plantation* was _____.

10. _____ was banished from the Massachusetts Bay Colony after criticizing
    Puritan ministers for overemphasizing good works as a goal in life.

Multiple Choice: Select the response that best answers each question or best completes each sentence.

1. All of the following contributed to the Pueblo Revolt of 1680 except:
    a. the Spanish forced the Pueblos to labor for the colonial elite.
    b. the region was racked by rampant epidemic disease.
    c. Spanish missionaries attempted to stamp out traditional Pueblo religious practices.
    d. the Pueblos interpreted repeated tremors as a divine signal to revolt.

2. French and Spanish American colonies differed from those of England:
    a. because the French and Spanish settlements experienced much more cultural mixing between Europeans
    and natives.
    b. because the English demanded less land from native communities.
    c. in that the English were much more tolerant and established policies of inclusion, unlike the exclusion of
    France and Spain.
    d. since France and Spain placed greater emphasis on developing agricultural colonies and England created
    mercantile settlements.

3. French traders gained access to inland fur markets:
    a. by conquering large tracts of land throughout North America.
    b. by establishing small settlements and trading centers along the St. Lawrence River.
    c. through an alliance with the Iroquois Confederacy.
    d. because they always offered higher prices than the English.
4. The English colony of Jamestown was:
    a. funded by a group of London investors known as the Virginia Company.
    b. the first permanent European settlement in North America.
    c. saved by the timely marriage of John Smith and Pocahontas.
    d. immediately and violently opposed by the Powhatan Confederacy.

5. The "merchantable commodity" that was profoundly important to the development of the Chesapeake economy was?
    a. Fish.
    b. Rice.
    c. Sugar.
    d. Tobacco.

6. During the seventeenth century, most migrants to the Chesapeake colonies:
    a. were slaves taken out of Africa.
    b. came as indentured servants.
    c. arrived as members of large families.
    d. were wealthy landowners and planters.

7. Maryland differed from Virginia in that:
    a. it solely relied on free labor rather than indentured servants.
    b. during the late 1600s it abandoned tobacco cultivation in favor of sugar production.
    c. it was a proprietary colony and a haven for Catholics.
    d. Maryland never adopted the system of headright grants.

8. John Winthrop's goal of making Massachusetts Bay Colony a "city on a hill":
    a. was based on the military strategy of seizing the high ground.
    b. is the first clear step toward colonists declaring independence.
    c. refers to the Puritan goal of creating a religious society for England to emulate.
    d. led to the signing of the Mayflower Compact.

9. Which New England colony best exemplified the principles of religious tolerance and freedom of religion:
    a. Plymouth.
    b. Virginia.
    c. Massachusetts Bay.
    d. Rhode Island.

10. Seventeenth century New England differed from Virginia:
    a. because New England featured greater family stability.
    b. since peaceful Puritans avoided conflict with local Indians.
    c. in that Virginia's greater maturity gave it stronger local institutions and more community solidarity.
    d. because only Massachusetts had representative government.

11. The Puritans who settled in North America:
    a. placed little importance on education beyond teaching the Ten Commandments.
    b. believed education was critical and quickly established a sophisticated education system.
    c. insisted that only ministers needed an education.
    d. did not have families with them and saw no need to establish an education system.

12. The "holy experiment" of Quaker Pennsylvania was characterized by all of the following except:
    a. generally peaceful relations with local Indians during the life of William Penn.
    b. guarantees of religious freedom.
    c. efficient and organized settlement of the region.
    d. restrictions allowing only Quakers to settle within the colony.

13. Bacon's Rebellion in 1676:
    a. accelerated the transition to slave labor within the colony.
    b. slowed westward expansion in Virginia.

c. inaugurated a period of peaceful relations between colonists and Indians.

d. reflected the deep rift between Catholic and Protestant Virginians.

14. As a result of the Glorious Revolution, American colonists:

a. dismantled the Dominion of New England.

b. were granted full autonomy from direct English rule.

c. ended all royal colonies in North America.

d. learned to tolerate a Catholic monarchy in England.

15. The restoration of the Stuart Monarchy led to the creation or acquisition of which of the following proprietary colonies?:

a. New York, Pennsylvania, and Maryland.

b. Rhode Island, South Carolina, and Pennsylvania.

c. New Jersey, New York, and South Carolina.

d. Virginia, Massachusetts Bay, and New York.

Thought Questions: Think carefully about the following questions or comments. Your answers should prepare you to participate in class discussions or help you to write an effective essay. In both class discussions and essays you should always support the arguments you make by referring to specific examples and historical evidence. You may use the space provided to sketch out ideas or outline your response.

1. Describe the colonies established in New Mexico, New France, and New Netherland. What relationship did these colonial communities have with the Indian peoples who already inhabited the regions where these Europeans settled?

2. Compare and contrast life in the Chesapeake colonies and in the New England colonies. Why did the colonists who settled in these regions choose to develop the colonies as they did? What struggles did they face as they pursued their goals?

3. What were the developments that led to the creation of the proprietary colonies? How were these colonies similar to or different from the earlier English colonies in the Chesapeake or New England?

4.   What were the specific causes of the various civil uprisings and Indian wars of the late seventeenth century? How did those conflicts influence the history of what would become the United States?

Map Skills: These questions are based on the maps in the chapter. Please use the blank map provided here for your answers.

1. Use the map to identify Albuquerque, El Paso del Norte, Santa Fé, and Mexico City. Outline the extent of Spanish colonial holdings in Mexico and the Southwest as of 1700. Identify the Rio Grande on the map.

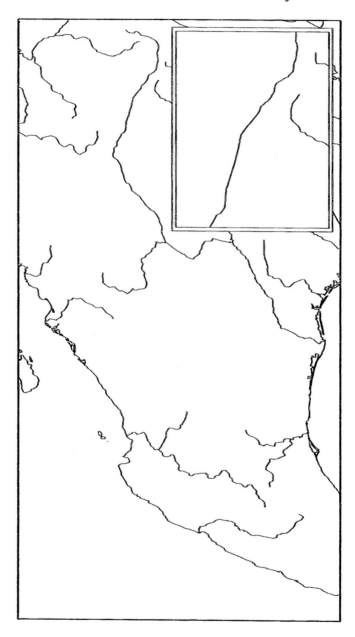

2. Locate the following regions of settlement: New France, New Sweden, New Netherland, Virginia, Maryland, and the Massachusetts Bay colonies.

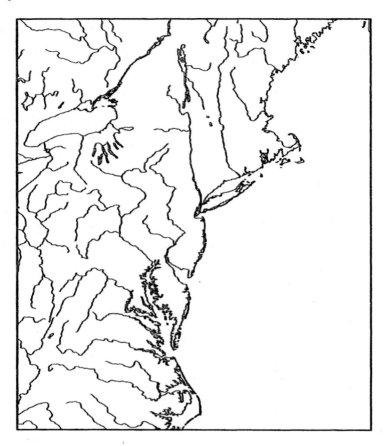

3. Indicate on the map the location of the following English colonies: New Hampshire, New York, Pennsylvania, New Jersey, Delaware, and Carolina.

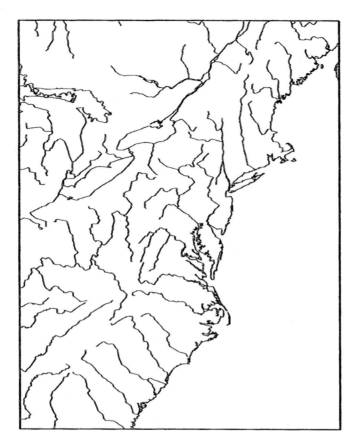

4. On the map above identify the following bodies of water: The St. Lawrence River, Lake Ontario, Lake Erie, Lake Huron, The Hudson River, Chesapeake Bay, and The James River.

Interpreting the Past

Name _____ Date _____

Analyze the relationship between the British North American colonies and the government back in England in light of the following documents.

DOCUMENT 1

Navigation Act of September 13, 1660
Source: http://www.founding.com/library/lbody.cfm?id=83&parent=17

For the increase of shipping and encouragement of the navigation of this nation wherein, under the good providence and protection of God, the wealth, safety, and strength of this kingdom is so much concerned; (2) be it enacted by the king's most excellent Majesty, and by the Lords and Commons in this present Parliament assembled, and by the authority thereof, that from and after the first day of December, one thousand six hundred and sixty, and from thence forward, no goods or commodities whatsoever shall be imported into or exported out of any lands, islands, plantations, or territories to his Majesty belonging or in his possession, or which may hereafter belong unto or be in the possession of his Majesty, his heirs, and successors, in Asia, Africa, or America, in any other ship or ships, vessel or vessels whatsoever, but in such ships or vessels as do truly and without fraud belong only to the people of England or Ireland, dominion of Wales or town of Berwick upon Tweed, or are of the built of and belonging to any the said lands, islands, plantations, or territories, as the proprietors and right owners thereof, and whereof the master and three fourths of the mariners at least are English; (3) under the penalty of the forfeiture and loss of all the goods and commodities which shall be imported into or exported out of any the aforesaid places in any other ship or vessel, as also of the ship or vessel, with all its guns, furniture, tackle, ammunition, and apparel; one third part thereof to his Majesty, his heirs and successors; one third part to the governor of such land, plantation, island, or territory where such default shall be committed, in case the said ship or goods be there seized, or otherwise that third part also to his Majesty, his heirs and successors; and the other third part to him or them who shall seize, inform, or sue for the same in any court of record, by bill, information, plaint, or other action, wherein no essoin, protection, or wager of law shall be allowed; (4) and all admirals and other commanders at sea of any the ships of war or other ship having commission from his Majesty or from his heirs or successors, are hereby authorized and strictly required to seize and bring in as prize all such ships or vessels as shall have offended contrary hereunto, and deliver them to the court of admiralty, there to be proceeded against; and in case of condensation, one moiety of such forfeitures shall be to the use of such admirals or commanders and their companies, to be divided and proportioned amongst them according to the rules and orders of the sea in case of ships taken prize; and the other moiety to the use of his Majesty, his heirs and successors XVIII. And it is further enacted by the authority aforesaid, that from and after the first day of April, which shall be in the year of our Lord one thousand six hundred sixty-one, no sugars, tobacco, cotton-wool, indigoes, ginger, rustic, or other dyeing wood, of the growth, production, or manufacture of any English plantations in America, Asia, or Africa, shall be shipped, carried, conveyed, or transported from any of the said English plantations to any land, island, territory, dominion, port, or place whatsoever, other than to such other English plantations as do belong to his Majesty, his heirs and successors, or to the kingdom of England or Ireland, or principality of Wales, or town of Berwick upon Tweed, there to be laid on shore; (2) under the penalty of the forfeiture of the said goods, or the full value thereof, as also of the ship, with all her guns, tackle, apparel, ammunition, and furniture; the one moiety to the king's Majesty, his heirs and successors, and the other moiety to him or them that shall seize, inform, or sue for the same in any court of record, by bill, plaint, or information, wherein no ession, protection, or wager of law shall be allowed.

DOCUMENT 2

Nathaniel Bacon's Challenge to William Berkeley (1676)
Source: A Hypertext on American History From the Colonial Period Until Modern Times,
http://odur.let.rug.nl/~usa/D/1651-1700/bacon_rebel/bacon_i.htm

The Declaration of the People.
1. For haveing upon specious pretences of publiqe works raised greate unjust taxes upon the Comonality for the advancement of private favorites and other sinister ends, but noe visible effects in any measure adequate, For not

36

haveing dureing this long time of his Gouvernement in any measure advanced this hopefull Colony either by fortificacons Townes or Trade.

2. For haveing abused and rendred contemptable the Magistrates of Justice, by advanceing to places of Judicature, scandalous and Ignorant favorites....

4. For haveing, protected, favoured, and Imboldned the Indians against his Majesties loyall subjects, never contriveing, requireing, or appointing any due or proper meanes of sattisfaction for theire many Invasions, robberies, and murthers comitted upon us.

5. For haveing when the Army of English, was just upon the track of those Indians, who now in all places burne, spoyle, murther and when we might with ease have destroyed them: who then were in open hostillity, for then haveing expressly countermanded, and sent back our Army, by passing his word for the peaceable demeanour of the said Indians, who imediately prosecuted theire evill intentions, comitting horred murthers and robberies in all places, being protected by the said engagement and word past of him the said Sir William Berkeley, haveing ruined and laid desolate a greate part of his Majesties Country, and have now drawne themselves into such obscure and remote places, and are by theire success soe imboldned and confirmed, by theire confederacy soe strengthned that the cryes of blood are in all places, and the terror, and constimation of the people soe greate, are now become, not onely a difficult, but a very formidable enimy, who might att first with ease have beene destroyed.

6. And lately when upon the loud outcryes of blood the Assembly had with all care raised and framed an Army for the preventing of further mischeife and safeguard of this his Majesties Colony....

These are therefore in his majesties name to command you forthwith to seize the persons above mentioned as Trayters to the King and Country and them to bring to Midle plantacon, and there to secure them untill further order, and in case of opposition, if you want any further assistance you are forthwith to demand itt in the name of the people in all the Counties of Virginia.

Nathaniel Bacon
Generall by Consent of the people.

DOCUMENT 3

William Berkeley's Response to Nathaniel Bacon (1676)
Source: A Hypertext on American History From the Colonial Period Until Modern Times,
http://odur.let.rug.nl/~usa/D/1651-1700/bacon_rebel/berke.htm

The declaration and Remonstrance of Sir William Berkeley his most sacred Majesties Governor and Captain Generall of Virginia...

And now I will state the Question betwixt me as a Governor and Mr. Bacon, and say that if any enimies should invade England, any Councellor Justice of peace or other inferiour officer, might raise what forces they could to protect his Majesties subjects, But I say againe, if after the Kings knowledge of this invasion, any the greatest peere of England, should raise forces against the kings prohibition this would be now, and ever was in all ages and Nations accompted treason. Nay I will goe further, that though this peere was truly zealous for the preservation of his King, and subjects, and had better and greater abibitys then all the rest of his fellow subjects, doe his King and Country service, yett if the King (though by false information) should suspect the contrary, itt were treason in this Noble peere to proceed after the King's prohibition, and for the truth of this I appeale to all the laws of England, and the Laws and constitutions of all other Nations in the world, And yett further itt is declared by this Parliament that the takeing up Armes for the King and Parliament is treason, for the event shewed that what ever the pretence was to seduce ignorant and well affected people, yett the end was ruinous both to King and people, as this will be if not prevented, I doe therefore againe declair that Bacon proceedeing against all Laws of all Nations modern and ancient, is Rebell to his sacred Majesty and this Country, nor will I insist upon the sweareing of men to live and dye togeather, which is treason by the very words of the Law.

To conclude, I have don what was possible both to friend and enimy, have granted Mr. Bacon three pardons, which he hath scornefully rejected, suppoaseing himselfe stronger to subvert then I and you to maineteyne the

Laws, by which onely and Gods assisting grace and mercy, all men mwt hope for peace and safety. I will add noe more though much more is still remaineing to Justifie me and condenme Mr. Bacon, but to desier that this declaration may be read in every County Court in the Country, and that a Court be presently called to doe itt, before the Assembly meet, That your approbation or dissattisfaction of this declaration may be knowne to all the Country, and the Kings Councell to whose most revered Judgments itt is submitted, Given the xxixth day of May, a happy day in the xxv"ith yeare of his most sacred Majesties Reigne, Charles the second, who God grant long and prosperously to Reigne, and lett all his good subjects say
Amen.
Sir William Berkeley
Governor

DOCUMENT 4

Edward Randolph Describes King Philip's War (1685)
Source: The American Colonist's Library, A Treasury of Primary Documents,
http://www.swarthmore.edu/SocSci/bdorsey/docs/45-ran.html

That notwithstanding the ancient law of the country, made in the year 1633, that no person should sell any armes or ammunition to any Indian upon penalty of £10 for every gun, £5 for a pound of powder, and 40s. for a pound of shot, yet the government of the Massachusets in the year 1657, upon designe to monopolize the whole Indian trade did publish and declare that the trade of furrs and peltry with the Indians in their jurisdiction did solely and properly belong to their commonwealth and not to every indifferent person, and did enact that no person should trade with the Indians for any sort of peltry, except such as were authorized by that court, under the penalty of £100 for every offence, giving liberty to all such as should have licence from them to sell, unto any Indian, guns, swords, powder and shot, paying to the treasurer 3d. for each gun and for each dozen of swords; 6d. for a pound of powder and for every ten pounds of shot, by which means the Indians have been abundantly furnished with great store of armes and ammunition to the utter ruin and undoing of many families in the neighbouring colonies to enrich some few of their relations and church members.

DOCUMENT 5

William Penn's Charter of Privileges (1701)
Source: The Avalon Project at the Yale Law School: Documents in Law, History and Diplomacy.
http://www.yale.edu/lawweb/avalon/states/pa07.htm

WILLIAM PENN, Proprietary and Governor of the Province of Pensilvania and Territories thereunto belonging, To all to whom these Presents shall come, sendeth Greeting. WHEREAS King CHARLES the Second, by His Letters Patents, under the Great Seal of England, bearing Date the Fourth Day of March in the Year One Thousand Six Hundred and Eighty-one, was graciously pleased to give and grant unto me, and my Heirs and Assigns for ever, this Province of Pennsilvania, with divers great Powers and Jurisdictions for the well Government thereof. AND WHEREAS the King's dearest Brother, JAMES Duke of YORK and ALBANY, &c. by his Deeds of Feoffment, under his Hand and Seal duly perfected, bearing Date the Twenty-Fourth Day of August, One Thousand Six Hundred Eighty and Two, did grant unto me, my Heirs and Assigns, all that Tract of Land, now called the Territories of Pensilvania, together with Powers and Jurisdictions for the good Government thereof. AND WHEREAS for the Encouragement of all the Freemen and Planters, that might be concerned in the said Province and Territories, and for the good Government thereof, I the said WILLIAM PENN, in the Year One Thousand Six Hundred Eighty and Three, for me, my Heirs and Assigns, did grant and confirm unto all the Freemen Planters and Adventurers therein, divers Liberties, Franchises and Properties, as by the said Grant, entituled, The FRAME of the Government of the Province of Pensilvania, and Territories thereunto belonging, in America, may appear; which Charter or Frame being found in some Parts of it, not so suitable to the present Circumstances of the Inhabitants, was in the Third Month, in the Year One Thousand Seven Hundred, delivered up to me, by Six Parts of Seven of the Freemen of this Province and Territories, in General Assembly met,

Provision being made in the said Charter, for that End and Purpose. AND WHEREAS I was then pleased to promise, That I would restore the said Charter to them again, with necessary Alterations, or in lieu thereof, give them another, better adapted to answer the present Circumstances and Conditions of the said Inhabitants; which they have now, by their Representatives in General Assembly met at Philadelphia, requested me to grant. KNOW YE THEREFORE, That for the further Well-being and good Government of the said Province, and Territories; and in Pursuance of the Rights and Powers before mentioned, I the said William Penn do declare, grant and confirm, unto all the Freemen, Planters and Adventurers, and other Inhabitants of this Province and Territories, these following Liberties, Franchises and Privileges, so far as in kme lieth, to be held, enjoyed and kept, by the Freemen, Planters and Adventurers, and other Inhabitants of and in the said Province and Territories "hereunto annexed, for ever.

DOCUMENT 6

The Closing of the Frontier (1763)
Source: The Solon Law Archive
http://www. solon.org/Constitutions/Canada/English/PreConfederation/rp_1763. html
also in Henry Steele Commager, ed., Documents of American History (New York: Appleton Century-Crofts, 1949), 47–50.

October 7, 1763
BY THE KING. A PROCLAMATION
Whereas We have taken into Our Royal Consideration the extensive and valuable Acquisitions in America, secured to our Crown by the late Definitive Treaty of Peace, concluded at Paris the 10th Day of February last; and being desirous that all Our loving Subjects, as well of our Kingdom as of our Colonies in America, may avail themselves with all convenient Speed, of the great Benefits and Advantages which must accrue therefrom to their Commerce, Manufactures, and Navigation, We have thought fit, with the Advice of our Privy Council, to issue this our Royal Proclamation, hereby to publish and declare to all our loving Subjects, that we have, with the Advice of our Said Privy Council, granted our Letters Patent, under our Great Seal of Great Britain, to erect, within the Countries and Islands ceded and confirmed to Us by the said Treaty, Four distinct and separate Governments, styled and called by the names of Quebec, East Florida, West Florida and Grenada, and limited and bounded as follows, viz....

We have also thought fit, with the advice of our Privy Council as aforesaid, to give unto the Governors and Councils of our said Three new Colonies, upon the Continent full Power and Authority to settle and agree with the Inhabitants of our said new Colonies or with any other Persons who shall resort thereto, for such Lands, Tenements and Hereditaments, as are now or hereafter shall be in our Power to dispose of; and them to grant to any such Person or Persons upon such Terms, and under such moderate Quit-Rents, Services and Acknowledgments, as have been appointed and settled in our other Colonies, and under such other Conditions as shall appear to us to be necessary and expedient for the Advantage of the Grantees, and the Improvement and settlement of our said Colonies.

DOCUMENT 7

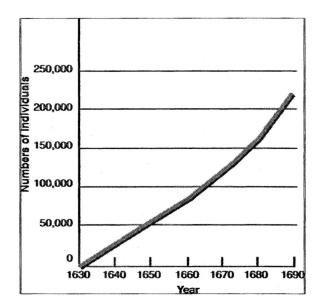

4. SLAVERY AND EMPIRE, 1441–1770

CHAPTER OVERVIEW

Summary

During the eighteenth century, slavery became a central feature of the successful development of European colonies throughout the Americas. In a place like Spanish New Mexico, Indians would fill the ranks of the enslaved, but the vast majority of unfree labor resulted from the nearly half-million Africans who were forcibly transported across the Atlantic Ocean. Those Africans who were fortunate enough to survive the horrors of the Middle Passage faced a life of continuing hardship in the tobacco, rice, and sugar plantations of the Americas. In this strange New World Africans labored extraordinarily hard for the benefit of the investors and planters who had enslaved them. While the enslaved were denied the fruits of their labor they did create riches of their own in the formation of an African American culture which greatly influenced and shaped the regions where they lived. While the formation of families and communities alleviated some of the suffering endured by the enslaved, they were far from content and would often rebel in an effort to obtain their freedom. Rebellion and the need to violently restrict the colonial slave populations was a stark reminder to slave holding societies that their wealth and freedom firmly rested on the exploitation and enslavement of others.

Focus Questions

1. How did the modern system of slavery develop?

2. What is the history of the slave trade and the Middle Passage?

3. How did Africans manage to create communities under the brutal slave system?

4. What were the connections between the institution of slavery and the imperial system of the eighteenth century?

5. How and why did racism develop in America?

CHAPTER REVIEW

Short Response: Consider these questions thoughtfully. Respond with the best possible short answer by filling in the blank.

1. The _____ took place in 1739 and was one of the most significant slave revolts in the history of North America.

2. The British corporation that held a monopoly over the slave trade to North America prior to 1698 was the
_____.

3. Slave Traders from the New England colony of _____ transported more than 100,000 enslaved Africans to the Americas.

4. The period of time in which enslaved Africans were carried across the sea in the holds of ships is known as the
_____.

5. The first Africans to arrive in British North America came ashore in the colony of
_____.

6. By the 1730s the slave population of the _____ became the first in the Western Hemisphere to achieve self-sustained growth.

7. _____ is credited with being the first person to introduce the cultivation of indigo to the Lower South.

8. In 1699 the Spanish governor of _____ declared it to be a refuge for runaway slaves from British colonies.

9. Quaker _____ *Considerations on the Keeping of Negroes* (1754) was the first anti-slavery publication in American history.

10. Large numbers of African and African American slaves were not converted to Christianity until after the
_____ which swept across the South just before the American Revolution.

Multiple Choice: Select the response that best answers each question or best completes each sentence.

1. One of the principal goals of the Stono Rebellion was:
   a. to disrupt tobacco production in nearby Virginia.
   b. for slaves to seize the city of Charles Town.
   c. to escape to Florida where the Spanish governor promised freedom to runaway English slaves.
   d. for slaves of Angolan ancestry to establish an independent settlement in the Appalachian Mountains.

2. All of the following were factors in the development of the African slave trade except:
   a. Portuguese trade relations with West African kingdoms.
   b. a tradition of using slave labor in sugar production.
   c. the European accord with Islamic states to outlaw enslaving Muslims.
   d. the reluctance of the Catholic Church to allow enslavement of Christians.

3. The majority of people who came to the Western Hemisphere prior to 1800 were from:
   a. Africa.
   b. England.
   c. Spain.
   d. France.

4. Of the 10 to 12 million enslaved Africans transported to the Americas:
    a. almost all were criminals or slaves within their own society.
    b. approximately 80% went to sugar producing Caribbean islands or Brazil.
    c. almost 50% were sent to mainland British North America.
    d. virtually all were captured in wars carried out by European slave raiding armies.

5. Which of the following best describes the Africans enslaved during the transatlantic slave trade:
    a. women outnumbered men by a ratio of two to one.
    b. physically mature adults over the age of 30 were preferred by planters and constituted most of the trade.
    c. most were sold by one or two kingdoms and were comprised of a relatively homogenous ethnic population.
    d. the vast majority were males aged 15 to 30.

6. All of the following were typical conditions or outcomes of the middle passage except:
    a. African mortality rates of greater than 25%.
    b. hot, cramped and unsanitary conditions in the hold.
    c. forced exercise on the ship's deck.
    d. numerous revolts and suicide attempts.

7. By 1770 Africans and African Americans living in British North America comprised:
    a. no more than 10% of the colonial population.
    b. over 50% of the workers in all colonies.
    c. more than 20% of the colonial population.
    d. a declining percentage of the total population.

8. During the colonial era of North America, slavery was:
    a. limited to the South.
    b. restricted to agriculture.
    c. on the decline everywhere.
    d. present in all areas.

9. Slave labor in the Lower South primarily was employed in the cultivation of:
    a. tobacco.
    b. sugar cane.
    c. rice and indigo.
    d. cotton.

10. Which of the following colonial religious groups was among the leaders of the fledgling antislavery movement:
    a. Quakers.
    b. Puritans.
    c. Pilgrims.
    d. Catholics.

11. The African American culture that emerged during the eighteenth century:
    a. was a mirror image of the dominant European colonial society around them.
    b. blended various African ethnic traditions with Indian and European forms to create a distinctive society.
    c. was an exact duplicate of the West African cultural environment.
    d. had no impact on the cultural development of white southerners.

12. Resistance to slavery:
    a. was minimal because Africans had been so traumatized by the middle passage.
    b. never crossed the slaves' minds because they were accustomed to slavery in Africa.

c. was worse in British North America than it was in Jamaica and Brazil.
d. usually took the form of running away or poor work in British North America.

13. Slavery was of vital importance to the British Empire
   a. because it is well known that Europeans cannot work in tropical environments.
   b. since there was no other way to fully populate its overseas colonies.
   c. because 95% of exports from the Americas to Great Britain came from its slave colonies of the South and Caribbean.
   d. since it made the colonies depend on the mother country for defense.

14. The port cities of the Northern colonies:
   a. were morally offended by slavery and resisted trade with Southern colonies.
   b. were forced by the British to trade in slave made goods.
   c. benefited tremendously from the slave trade and commercial relationships with slave colonies.
   d. were prevented by British mercantile policies from trading in profitable slave produced goods.

15. One of the great ironies of the history of slavery in America is:
   a. that few white Americans benefited from the institution.
   b. the reality that white freedom and prosperity rested on the enslavement of African Americans.
   c. that slavery eventually created an egalitarian colonial society.
   d. the fact that nobody really knows how the practice even started.

Thought Questions: Think carefully about the following questions or comments. Your answers should prepare you to participate in class discussions or help you to write an effective essay. In both class discussions and essays you should always support the arguments you make by referring to specific examples and historical evidence. You may use the space provided to sketch out ideas or outline your response.

1. Describe how the development of the rice, sugar, and tobacco industries shaped the creation and presence of slavery in the Americas. Were there any differences in the structure of slavery within the regions committed to these various commodities?

2. Discuss the process Africans experienced as they were enslaved, as they were transported to America, and as they arrived in specific colonies.

3. Describe the development of the African American community in the Americas? In what ways were Africans transformed by their new environment and what impact did the enslaved have upon the transformation of the New World?

4. How did the African slave system influence the advent and growth of the British Empire? What was the relationship of colonists to the institution of slavery?

5. What were the implications of slavery for the concepts of liberty and freedom that were emerging in Britain's North American colonies?

Map Skills: These questions are based on the maps in the chapter. Please use the blank map provided here for your answers.

1. Locate the following colonies that relied heavily on slave labor: the Chesapeake, Cuba, Hispaniola, the Lower South, Spanish Florida, and Louisiana.

2. Identify the three legs of the "Triangular Trade" across the Atlantic Ocean, and indicate briefly the commodities transported on each portion of the trade.

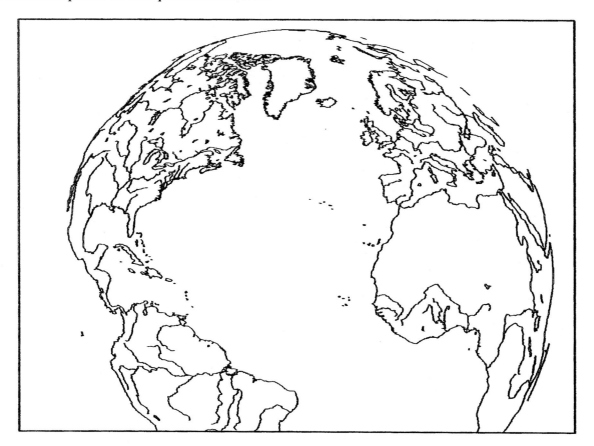

3. On the map above identify the following major regions of the African slave trade: Senegambia, Winward Coast, Gold Coast, Bight of Benin, Bight of Biafra, West Central Africa.

Interpreting the Past

Name _____ **Date** _____

Explain the process by which slavery was created in North America.

DOCUMENT 1

DOCUMENT 2

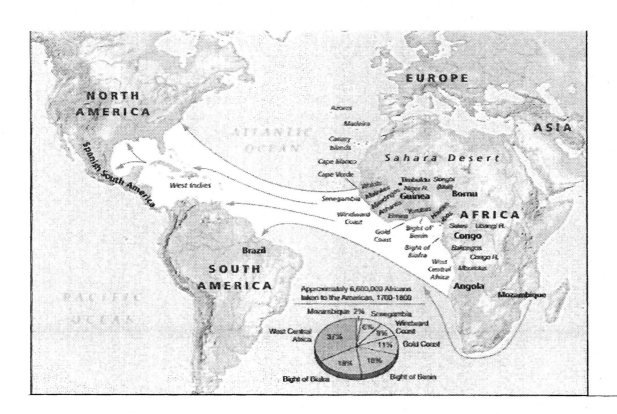

DOCUMENT 3

Source: Alexander Falconbridge, The African Slave Trade (1788)

... ABOUT EIGHT O'CLOCK IN THE MORNING THE NEGROES ARE GENERALLY BROUGHT UPON DECK. THEIR IRONS BEING EXAMINED, A LONG CHAIN, WHICH IS LOCKED TO A RING-BOLT, FIXED IN THE DECK, IS RUN THROUGH THE RINGS OF THE SHACKLES OF THE MEN, AND THEN LOCKED TO ANOTHER RING-BOLT, FIXED ALSO IN THE DECK. BY THIS MEANS FIFTY OR SIXTY, AND SOMETIMES MORE, ARE FASTENED TO ONE CHAIN, IN ORDER TO PREVENT THEM FROM RISING, OR ENDEAVORING TO ESCAPE. IF THE WEATHER PROVES FAVORABLE, THEY ARE PERMITTED TO REMAIN IN THAT SITUATION TILL FOUR OR FIVE IN THE AFTERNOON, WHEN THEY ARE DISENGAGED FROM THE CHAIN, AND SENT DOWN. ... UPON THE NEGROES REFUSING TO TAKE SUSTENANCE, I HAVE SEEN COALS OF FIRE, GLOWING HOT, PUT ON A SHOVEL, AND PLACED SO NEAR THEIR LIPS, AS TO SCORCH AND BURN THEM. AND THIS HAS BEEN ACCOMPANIED WITH THREATS, OF FORCING THEM TO SWALLOW THE COALS, IF THEY ANY LONGER PERSISTED IN REFUSING TO EAT. THESE MEANS HAVE GENERALLY HAD THE DESIRED EFFECT. I HAVE ALSO BEEN CREDIBLY INFORMED THAT A CERTAIN CAPTAIN IN THE SLAVE TRADE POURED MELTED LEAD ON SUCH OF THE NEGROES AS OBSTINATELY REFUSED THEIR FOOD. EXERCISE BEING DEEMED NECESSARY FOR THE PRESERVATION OF THEIR HEALTH, THEY ARE SOMETIMES OBLIGATED TO DANCE, WHEN THE WEATHER WILL PERMIT THEIR COMING ON DECK. IF THEY GO ABOUT IT RELUCTANTLY, OR DO NOT MOVE WITH AGILITY, THEY ARE FLOGGED; A PERSON STANDING BY THEM ALL THE TIME WITH AT CAT-O'-NINE-TAILS IN HIS HAND FOR THAT PURPOSE.

DOCUMENT 4

Source: Olaudah Equiano, The Middle Passage (1788)

... I and some few more slaves, that were not saleable amongst the rest, from very much fretting, were shipped off in a sloop for North America. ... While I was in this plantation [in Virginia] the gentleman, to whom I suppose the estate belonged, being unwell, I was one day sent for to his dwelling house to fan him; when I came into the room where he was I was very much affrighted at some things I saw, and the more so as I had seen a black woman slave as I came through the house, who was cooking the dinner, and the poor creature was cruelly loaded with various kinds of iron machines; she had one particularly on her head, which locked her mouth so fast that she could scarcely speak; and could not eat nor drink. I was much astonished and shocked at this contrivance, which I afterwards learned was called the iron muzzle ...

DOCUMENT 5

An Act Concerning Servants and Slaves
Source: William Waller Hening, The Statutes at Large; Being a Collection of all the Laws of Virginia, from the First Session of the Legislature in the Year 1619, (New York: R & W & G. Bartow, 1823). Vol. I.
http://www.law.du.edu/russell/lh/alh/docs/virginiaslaverystatutes.html

IV. And also be it enacted, by the authority aforesaid, and it is hereby enacted, That all servants imported and brought into this country, by sea or land, who were not Christians in their native country, (except Turks and Moors in amity with her majesty, and others that can make due proof of their being free in England, or any other Christian country, before they were shipped, in order to transportation hither) shall be accounted and be slaves, and as such be here bought and sold notwithstanding a conversion to Christianity afterwards.
V. And be it enacted, by the authority aforesaid, and it is hereby enacted, That if any person or persons shall hereafter import into this colony, and here sell as a slave, any person or persons that shall have been a freeman in

any Christian country, island, or plantation, such importer and seller as aforesaid, shall forfeit and pay, to the party from whom the said freeman shall recover his freedom, double the sum for which the said freeman was sold. To be recovered, in any court of record within this colony, according to the course of the common law, wherein the defendant shall not be admitted to plead in bar, any act or statute for limitation of actions.

VI. Provided always, that a slave's being in England, shall not be sufficient to discharge him of his slavery, without other proof of his being manumitted there.

DOCUMENT 6

James Oglethorpe: The Stono Rebellion (1739)
Source: James Oglethorpe: The Stono Rebellion (1739), Allen Chandler, ed., The Colonial Records of the State of Georgia, vol. 22 (Atlanta: Chas. P. Byrd Press, 1913), pp. 232–236.

Sometime since there was a Proclamation published at Augustine, in which the King of Spain (then at Peace with Great Britain) promised Protection and Freedom to all Negroes Slaves that would resort thither. Certain Negroes belonging to Captain Davis escaped to Augustine, and were received there. They were demanded by General Oglethorpe who sent Lieutenant Demere to Augustine, and the Governour assured the General of his sincere Friendship, but at the same time showed his Orders from the Court of Spain, by which he was to receive all Run away Negroes... On the 9th day of September last being Sunday which is the day the Planters allow them to work for themselves, Some Angola Negroes assembled, to the number of Twenty; and one who was called Jemmy was their Captain, they suprized a Warehouse belonging to Mr. Hutchenson at a place called Stonehow [sicÑ]; they there killed Mr. Robert Bathurst, and Mr. Gibbs, plundered the House and took a pretty many small Arms and Powder, which were there for Sale. Next they plundered and burnt Mr. Godfrey's house, and killed him, his Daughter and Son. They then turned back and marched Southward along Pons Pons, which is the Road through Georgia to Augustine, they passed Mr. Wallace's Taxern towards day break, and said they would not hurt him, for he was a good Man and kind to his Slaves, but they broke open and plundered Mr. Lemy's House, and killed him, his wife and Child. They marched on towards Mr. Rose's resolving to kill him; but he was saved by a Negroe, who having hid him went out and pacified the others. Several Negroes joyned them, they calling out Liberty, marched on with Colours displayed, and two Drums beating, pursuing all the white people they met with, and killing Man Woman and Child when they could come up to them...The Lieutenant Governour sent an account of this to General Oglethorpe, who met the advices on his return form the Indian Nation He immediately ordered a Troop of Rangers to be ranged, to patrole through Georgia, placed some Men in the Garrison at Palichocolas, which was before abandoned, and near which the Negroes formerly passed, being the only place where Horses can come to swim over the River Savannah for near 100 miles, ordered out the Indians in pursuit, and a Detachment of the Garrison at Port Royal to assist the Planters on any Occasion, and published a Proclamation ordering all the Constables &c. of Georgia to pursue and seize all Negroes, with a Reward for any that should be taken. It is hoped these measures will prevent any Negroes from getting down to the Spaniards.

DOCUMENT 7

Jefferson, the Slaveowner
Source: Thomas Jefferson, advertisement, *Virginia Gazette*, September 14, 1769.

Run away from the subscriber in Albemarle, a Mulatto slave called Sandy, about 35 years of age, his stature is rather low, inclining to corpulence, and his complexion light; he is a shoemaker by trade, in which he uses his left hand principally, can do coarse carpenters work, and is something of a horse jockey; he is greatly addicted to drink, and when drunk is insolent and disorderly, in his conversation he swears much, and in his behavior is artful and knavish. He took with him a white horse, much scarred with traces, of which it is expected he will endeavor to dispose; he also carried his shoemakers tools, and will probably endeavor to get employment that way.
Whoever conveys the said slave to me, in Albemarle, shall have 40 s. reward, if taken up within the county, 4 l. if elsewhere within the colony, and 10 l. if in any other colony, from Thomas Jefferson.

5. THE CULTURES OF COLONIAL NORTH AMERICA, 1700–1780

CHAPTER OVERVIEW

Summary

The eighteenth century witnessed a blossoming of specific regional cultures throughout North America. In most cases these developing societies were expansionist in nature and placed increasing pressure on Indian peoples who had already faced significant changes in their ways of life. European colonies also faced change as increasing numbers of immigrants, both forced and free, began to arrive in North America. Some colonies reacted to this influx by attempting to enforce homogeneity, while others opened their doors to the cultures and profits that the new arrivals generated. As colonies expanded, European rivalries also increased as the French, Spanish, and English each sought to dominate a growing portion of the continent. Pastors and other intellectuals also fought for a share of the hearts and minds of the colonial populations as the ideas of the enlightenment, and a powerful religious revival, squared off in the New World.

Focus Questions

1. What were the similarities and differences among eighteenth-century Spanish, French, and British colonies?

2. What was the impact on British culture of increasing European immigration?

3. In what ways did Indian America change as a result of contact with European customs and life ways?

4. What were the patterns of work and class in eighteenth-century North America?

5. How did tension between Enlightenment thought and traditional culture lead to the Great Awakening?

CHAPTER REVIEW

Short Response: Consider these questions thoughtfully. Respond with the best possible short answer by filling in the blank.

1. The minister who helped lead the religious revival in the Puritan town of Northampton during the 1730s was

_____.

2. The major religious revival that swept throughout many parts of British North America is known as the

_____.

3. The _____ formed the periphery of the largest and most prosperous European colony on the North American continent, the Viceroyalty of New Spain.

4. The _____ stretched from the mouth of the St. Lawrence River southwest through the Great Lakes, then down the Mississippi River to the Gulf of Mexico.

5. The English political philosopher _____ wrote "A Letter Concerning Tolerance," in 1689.

6. _____ was a Quaker colony that some called a "heaven for farmers."

7. The colonial region known for its rugged egalitarianism and disdain for rank was the

_____.

8. Landowning farmers of small to moderate means, artisans, craftsmen, and small shopkeepers were all part of the _____ which comprised the greatest portion of British North America's free population.

9. Prime Minister _____ helped cultivate traditions of colonial self-government when he assumed that a decentralized administration of the British colonies would best accomplish the nation's economic goals.

10. To educated eighteenth century Britons, the word _____ implied mob rule which is why most colonial governments were the domain of the elite.

Multiple Choice: Select the response that best answers each question or best completes each sentence.

1. The Great Awakening is best described as:
    a. an intellectual revolution that focused on empirical study.
    b. the moment when colonists decided to declare independence from Britain.
    c. a religious revival that led to increased church membership.
    d. a period of peace between colonists and the Indians of New England.

2. Each of the following is a typical way that Indian peoples adapted to the new colonial environment except:
    a. used firearms.
    b. participated in the commercial economy.
    c. adopted metal tools.
    d. cut off ties with Europeans to prevent further epidemics.

3. In reaction to the growing presence of rival colonial empires in North America, the Spanish:
    a. retreated to defensible boundaries within New Spain.
    b. negotiated a mutual defense treaty with England.
    c. founded new northern outposts like the missions of California.
    d. accepted defeat and withdrew entirely from North America.

4. The French Crescent refers to:
    a. the French colonial presence stretching from the St. Lawrence River to the Great Lakes to New Orleans.
    b. a popular roll eaten by fur traders in the backcountry.
    c. a half circle of Caribbean sugar islands controlled by France.
    d. the most productive agricultural lands in French Canada.

5. Which colonial leader argued for religious tolerance by proclaiming "Forced Worship…stinks in God's nostrils":
    a. Jonathan Edwards.
    b. Roger Williams.
    c. John Winthrop.
    d. William Bradford.

6. In comparison to New England, the Middle Colonies:
    a. were made up of an ethnically homogenous population.
    b. had some of the poorest soil for farming in the North.
    c. were a veritable mosaic of ethnic and religious communities.
    d. had a harder time attracting immigrants..

7. Because of the labor intensive requirements of growing tobacco, Chesapeake farms:
    a. were much larger than those along the rice coast.
    b. looked more like Caribbean plantations than those of South Carolina.
    c. were smaller on average than those of the rice coast.
    d. soon abandoned tobacco and planted rice and indigo like South Carolina.

8. Most colonists throughout North America shared many common characteristics including:
    a. the importance of oral culture, an attachment to community, and a commitment to agriculture.
    b. an absolute commitment to Protestantism and the dominance of manufacturing.
    c. a passion for risk-taking entrepreneurial activity.
    d. a strong desire to escape the confining traditions of their homelands.

9. One of the primary differences between life in Europe and North America was:
    a. the general social equality that existed in the colonies.
    b. the abundance of cheap land in the colonies.
    c. that colonial women enjoyed numerous opportunities outside of the household.
    d. that wage laborers in the colonies were plentiful and worked for lower pay.

10. One reason why the English colonies grew faster than those of the Spanish and French was because:
    a. the Spanish and French colonies had low fertility rates.
    b. only the English had low mortality rates.
    c. the English had less restrictive rules on immigration.
    d. the French only allowed the Huguenots to immigrate to the colonies.

11. What percentage of the English colonial population would have been of the "middling sort?":
    a. Less than 10% of the total population.
    b. More than half of the total population.
    c. None could qualify for such a high status.
    d. Only those living in middle colonies were eligible.

12. The Anglican minister who helped spread the Great Awakening throughout the English colonies was:
    a. Ethan Frost.
    b. Washington Gladden.

c. John Wesley.
d. George Whitefield.

13. According to Enlightenment thinkers:
    a. the universe is governed by natural laws.
    b. the mysterious, and unpredictable whims of God shape daily events.
    c. God only selected a handful of souls to receive eternal salvation.
    d. the only way to understand the world is to read the Bible.

14. During the eighteenth century, most colonial assemblies:
    a. collected local revenues, approved the appointment of officials, and controlled the "purse strings."
    b. lost most of their power to English appointed governors.
    c. were abandoned because of rampant corruption.
    d. were elected by fewer than 20% of the white male population.

15. According to some historians, the struggle between New Light and Old Lights in Connecticut:
    a. reflected the increasing tension between the land hungry Puritans and Indians.
    b. centered on the decline of religious enthusiasm brought on by the Enlightenment.
    c. helped create leaders who contributed to the American Revolution.
    d. made the region vulnerable to French territorial ambitions.

Thought Questions: Think carefully about the following questions or comments. Your answers should prepare you to participate in class discussions or help you to write an effective essay. In both class discussions and essays you should always support the arguments you make by referring to specific examples and historical evidence. You may use the space provided to sketch out ideas or outline your response.

1. Describe the characteristics of the cultures that emerged in the British colonies, the French Crescent, and the Spanish Borderlands. How and why did these regions differ from one another?

2. Describe what would life be like for an English settler, who migrated to British North America in the eighteenth century. Select one of the following regions to describe: New England, the Middle Colonies, the Backcountry, or the South. What, if anything, made this region unique?

3. Discuss the circumstances and events that led to diverging social, economic, and political patterns in eighteenth-century British America. What were the biggest changes that developed in British North America since the seventeenth century?

4. What were the concepts advanced by the Enlightenment and by the Great Awakening? What are the differences between the two movements? Describe any similarities that existed.

Map Skills: These questions are based on the maps in the chapter. Please use the blank map provided here for your answers.

1. Identify these important regions in eighteenth-century North America: the Backcountry, the Chesapeake, the Lower South, New England, the French Crescent, and the Spanish Borderlands.

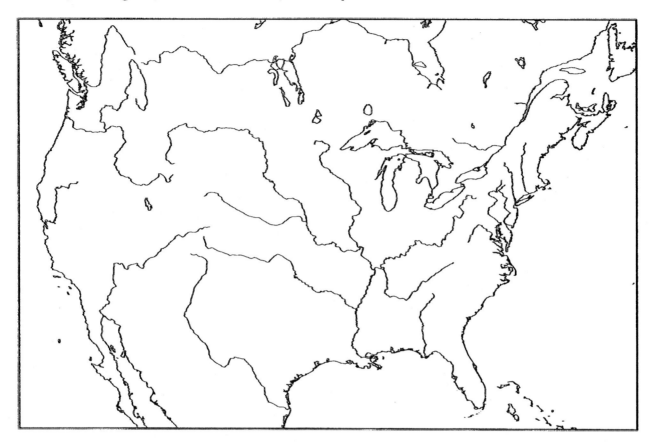

2. Locate the areas where the following ethnic groups were most concentrated by 1790: African, Dutch, English and Welsh, German and Swiss, Scots Highlanders, and Scots-Irish. Which of these areas reflects the greatest cultural diversity? What regions were less diverse and what helps explain these differences?

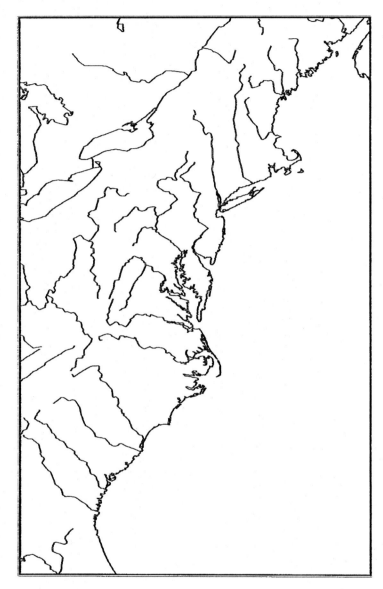

Interpreting the Past

Name _____ Date _____

Defend or refute the following statement: Differing patterns of immigration and migration created different social and political climates in the various regions of the Americas.

DOCUMENT 1

Source: J. Hector St. John Crèvecoeur, "What Is an American?" (1782)

The next wish of this traveller will be to know whence came all these people? They are a mixture of English, Scotch, Irish, French, Dutch, Germans, and Swedes. From this promiscuous breed, that race now called Americans have arisen. The eastern provinces must indeed be excepted, as being the unmixed descendants of Englishmen. I have heard many wish that they had been more intermixed also: for my part, I am no wisher, and think it much better as it has happened. They exhibit a most conspicuous figure in this great and variegated picture; they too enter for a great share in the pleasing perspective displayed in these thirteen provinces. I know it is fashionable to reflect on them, but I respect them for what they have done, for the accuracy and wisdom with which they have settled their territory; for the decency of their manners; for their early love of letters; their ancient college, the first in this hemisphere; for their industry; which to me who am but a farmer, is the criterion of everything. There never was a people, situated as they are, who with so ungrateful a soil have done more in so short a time. Do you think that the monarchical ingredients which are more prevalent in other governments, have purged them from all foul stains? Their histories assert the contrary.

DOCUMENT 2

Source: Benjamin Franklin, "Observations Concerning the Increase of Mankind, Peopling of Countries, &c." (1751)

There is in short, no Bound to the prolific Nature of Plants or Animals, but what is made by their crowding and interfering with each others Means of Subsistence. Was the Face of the Earth vacant of other Plants, it might be gradually sowed and overspread with one Kind only; as, for Instance, with Fennel; and were it empty of other Inhabitants, it might in a few Ages be replenish'd from one Nation only; as, for Instance, with Englishmen. Thus there are suppos'd to be now upwards of One Million English Souls in North-America, (tho' 'tis thought scarce 80,000 have been brought over Sea) and yet perhaps there is not one the fewer in Britain, but rather many more, on Account of the Employment the Colonies afford to Manufacturers at Home. This Million doubling, suppose but once in 25 Years, will in another Century be more than the People of England, and the greatest Number of Englishmen will be on this Side the Water. What an Accession of Power to the British Empire by Sea as well as Land! What Increase of Trade and Navigation! What Number of Ships and Seamen! We have been here but little more than 100 Years, and yet the Force of our Privateers in the late War, united, was greater, both in Men and Guns, than that of the whole British Navy in Queen Elizabeth's Time. . . .

   And since Detachments of English from Britain sent to America, will have their Places at Home so soon supply'd and increase so largely here; why should the Palatine Boors be suffered to swarm into our Settlements, and by herding together establish their Language and Manners to the Exclusion of ours? Why should Pennsylvania, founded by the English, become a Colony of Aliens, who will shortly be so numerous as to Germanize us instead of our Anglifying them, and will never adopt our Language or Customs, any more than they can acquire our Complexion.

DOCUMENT 3

DOCUMENT 4

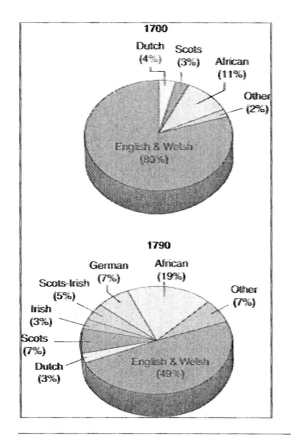

DOCUMENT 5

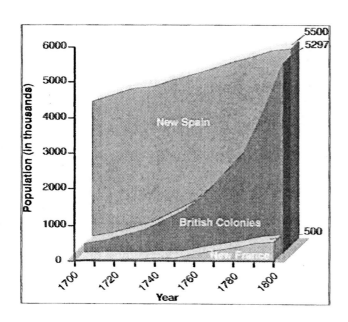

DOCUMENT 6

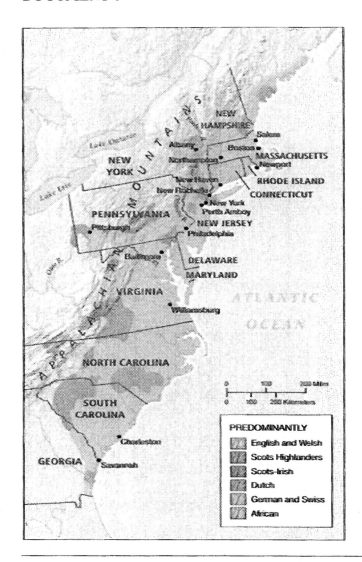

DOCUMENT 7

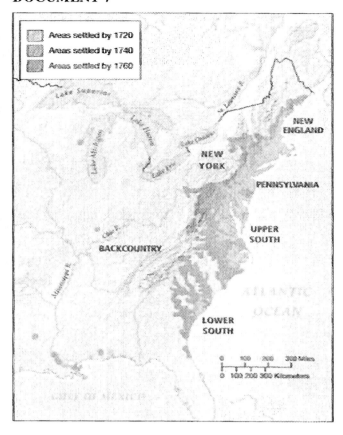

6. FROM EMPIRE TO INDEPENDENCE, 1750–1776

CHAPTER OVERVIEW

Summary

At the conclusion of the Seven Years' War, Britain rode high on a wave of colonial success and seemed poised to consolidate its gains in North America. However, the seeds of colonial dissolution were contained in the same victory the British celebrated. Distance, experience, and competing views about governance led British colonists to resist England's efforts to make the colonies operate more efficiently for the mother country. Repeated disputes over new British policies augmented a growing sense of American nationalism and triggered a long string of colonial protests. In time, thirteen separate and differing colonies managed to form a unified front against the British, and when England refused to relent in her interpretation of the colonial relationship, the Americans chose independence rather than to continue as part of the British Empire.

Focus Questions

1. What were the conflicts that led to the Seven Years' War, and what were the outcomes for Great Britain, France, and the American Indians?

2. Why did American nationalism develop in the aftermath of the French and Indian War?

3. What was Great Britain's changing policy toward its North American colonies in the 1760s?

4. What were the assumptions of American republicanism?

5. How did the colonies attempt to achieve unity in their confrontation with Great Britain?

CHAPTER REVIEW

Short Response: Consider these questions thoughtfully. Respond with the best possible short answer by filling in the blank.

1. The First Continental Congress was held in _____ during September of 1774.

2. At the Continental Congress, _____ exuberantly declared that "The distinctions between Virginians, Pennsylvanians, New Yorkers, and New Englanders, are no more...I am not a Virginian, but an American."

3. In 1754 British colonial leaders failed to achieve greater unity among the colonies at the

_____ .

4. The expulsion of French speaking Acadians from territory the British took from France led to a migration to Louisiana where the descendants of these migrants became know as _____ .

5. The Seven Years War was legally ended in 1763 by the _____ .

6. The British _____ declared the trans-Appalachian region to be "Indian Country."

7. _____ , written by John Trenchard and Thomas Gordon, was among the popular literature of British North America that led colonists to question English rule.

8. _____ was a brilliant Massachusetts lawyer who asserted that "No government" could rightfully deprive a man of the right "to his life, his liberty, and his property."

9. In 1764 the English passed the _____ which actually reduced the tariff charged on imported sugar.

10. Opposition to the Stamp Act was most violent in the city of _____ where the home of Lt. Governor Hutchinson was ransacked.

Multiple Choice: Select the response that best answers each question or best completes each sentence.

1. An important task facing the First Continental Congress was:
    a. defining the issues that would justify a declaration of independence from England.
    b. emphasizing the common cause Americans had without compromising local identities.
    c. funding the ongoing war that the patriots were fighting against the British military.
    d. creating a form of republican government that would ensure a more perfect union.

2. The Albany Conference of 1754:
    a. was an attempt to wipe out the Iroquois Confederacy.
    b. marked the first open split between Great Britain and the American colonies.
    c. led to the Declaration of Independence.
    d. was an effort to promote greater cooperation between British colonies.

3. Which of the following were points of contention between England and France that led to the Seven Years' War?:
    a. the North Atlantic Coast (Nova Scotia).
    b. the Great Lakes region between New France and New York.
    c. the Ohio Country.
    d. All of the Above.

4. During the Seven Years' War:
    a. the Indian peoples of North Amerca declared neutrality.
    b. the French and English both successfully recruited Indian allies to assist them.

c. only the French were able to attract Indian allies.

d. the English rejected any aid offered to them by potential Indian allies.

5. The British policy which prohibited English colonists from moving beyond the crest of the Appalachian Mountains was the:

a. Appalachian Decree of 1763.

b. Indian Removal Program of 1765.

c. Royal Proclamation of 1763.

d. Treaty of Fort Stanwix.

6. Under the Treaty of Paris:

a. Britain lost any claim to the Ohio Territory to France.

b. France was forced to cede all of its North American territories to England and Spain.

c. Spain was allowed to retain Florida.

d. France retained control of Louisiana but had to relinquish its claim to Canada.

7. The idea of republicanism:

a. led to the formation of the oldest continuous party in the United States.

b. asserted that the truly just society provided the greatest liberty to individuals.

c. was rejected by most colonists as being too impractical.

d. supported the belief that Monarchs were need to keep the mob in check.

8. During the 1760s, the main American weapon of resistance to British policy was:

a. economic boycotts.

b. military action.

c. political petitions.

d. violent demonstrations.

9. The Boston Massacre in 1770 was:

a. a heinous act of British violence committed against all of the American people.

b. an unfortunate and tragic incident that developed out of numerous colonial tensions.

c. the most violent act ever committed by American Indians against the British colonies.

d. the event that led to an immediate break with England and American independence.

10. The Stamp Act:

a. was generally well received by colonists.

b. placed high import duties on sugar and rum.

c. led to widespread protests and violence in the colonies.

d. A & B.

11. The English response to the Boston Tea Party was the:

a. Force Bill.

b. Declaratory Act.

c. Coercive Acts.

d. Quartering Bill.

12. The Tea Act of 1773:

a. actually made the price of tea cheaper in the colonies.

b. made tea so expensive that only the wealthy could drink it.

c. granted control of the sale of tea to Dutch interests linked to the crown.

d. generated the development of tea plantations in backcountry Pennsylvania.

13. The Quebec Act offended many British colonists because:
    a. it created an authoritarian governing structure on the territory.
    b. it granted religious toleration to the Roman Catholic Church.
    c. it did not allow for an elected council or legislature.
    d. all of the above.

14. The pamphlet that reshaped American popular thinking about independence was:
    a. *Letters from a Farmer in Pennsylvania* by John Dickinson.
    b. *A Seditious Libel* by John Peter Zenger.
    c. *Give Me Liberty or Give Me Death* by Patrick Henry.
    d. *Common Sense* by Thomas Paine.

15. The Second Continental Congress
    a. rejected the idea of sending King George an "Olive Branch Petition" in 1775.
    b. sought no assistance from other British colonies.
    c. voted in favor of declaring independence on July 2, 1776.
    d. pushed Thomas Jefferson to criticize the king for encouraging slavery.

Thought Questions: Think carefully about the following questions or comments. Your answers should prepare you to participate in class discussions or help you to write an effective essay. In both class discussions and essays you should always support the arguments you make by referring to specific examples and historical evidence. You may use the space provided to sketch out ideas or outline your response.

1. What was the outcome of the Seven Years' War and how did this conflict impact the lives of the colonists in British North America? How did this war help create American nationalism?

2. Why were colonists so angry about the Royal Proclamation of 1763? How did British colonists respond to this policy?

3. How did American colonists understand the eighteenth century idea of republicanism? What are the principles embodied in republicanism, and how might they be likely to contribute to suspicion of or resistance to government?

4. What were the most important points of disagreement between England and her North American colonies from 1763 to 1776? Why did it take the colonies over a decade to declare independence? What does this delay tell us about the colonies, if anything.

Map Skills: These questions are based on the maps in the chapter. Please use the blank map provided here for your answers.

1. Indicate the colonial boundaries of the French, English, and Spanish that resulted from the Treaty of Paris in 1763. In addition, draw the Proclamation Line of 1763 on the map.

2. Following the Quebec Act of 1774, where were the borders of Quebec, the Indian Country, and Louisiana?

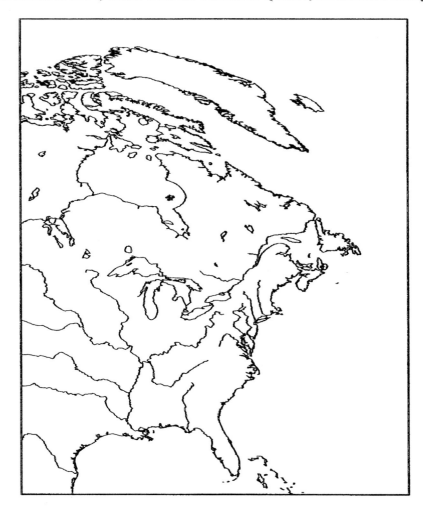

Interpreting the Past

Name _____ Date _____

Explain and assess the underlying cause or causes of the American Revolution. Which, if any, were the most significant and why?

DOCUMENT 1

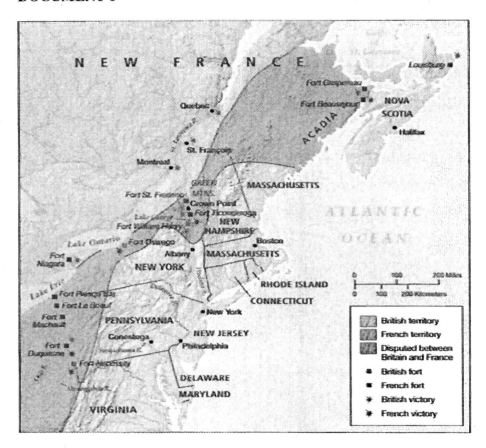

DOCUMENT 2

Source: Benjamin Franklin, Testimony Against the Stamp Act (1766)

Q. For what purposes are those taxes laid?

A. For the support of the civil and military establishments of the country, and to discharge the heavy debt contracted in the last [Seven Years'] war. . . .

Q. Are not all the people very able to pay those taxes?

A. No. The frontier counties, all along the continent, have been frequently ravaged by the enemy and greatly impoverished, are able to pay very little tax. . . .

Q. Are not the colonies, from their circumstances, very able to pay the stamp duty?

A. In my opinion there is not gold and silver enough in the colonies to pay the stamp duty for one year.

Q. Don't you know that the money arising from the stamps was all to be laid out in America?

A. I know it is appropriated by the act to the American service; but it will be spent in the conquered colonies, where the soldiers are, not in the colonies that pay it. . . .

Q. Do you think it right that America should be protected by this country and pay no part of the expense?

A. That is not the case. The colonies raised, clothed, and paid, during the last war, near 25,000 men, and spent many millions.

Q. Where you not reimbursed by Parliament?

A. We were only reimbursed what, in your opinion, we had advanced beyond our proportion, or beyond what might reasonably be expected from us; and it was a very small part of what we spent. Pennsylvania, in particular, disbursed about 500,000 pounds, and the reimbursements, in the whole, did not exceed 60,000 pounds. . . .

Q. Do you think the people of America would submit to pay the stamp duty, if it was moderated?

A. No, never, unless compelled by force of arms. . . .

Q. What was the temper of America towards Great Britain before the year 1763?

A. The best in the world. They submitted willingly to the government of the Crown, and paid, in all their courts, obedience to acts of Parliament. . . .

Q. What is your opinion of a future tax, imposed on the same principle with that of the Stamp Act? How would the Americans receive it?

A. Just as they do this. They would not pay it.

Q. Have not you heard of the resolutions of this House, and of the House of Lords, asserting the right of Parliament relating to America, including a power to tax the people there?

A. Yes, I have heard of such resolutions.

Q. What will be the opinion of the Americans on those resolutions?

A. They will think them unconstitutional and unjust.

Q. Was it an opinion in America before 1763 that the Parliament had no right to lay taxes and duties there?

A. I never heard any objection to the right of laying duties to regulate commerce; but a right to lay internal taxes was never supposed to be in Parliament, as we are not represented there. . . .

DOCUMENT 3

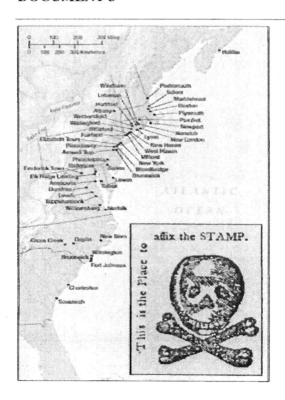

DOCUMENT 4

Source: The Boston "Massacre" or Victims of Circumstance? (1770)

Thirty or forty persons, mostly lads, being by this means gathered in King Street, Capt. Preston with a party of men with charged bayonets, came from the main guard to the commissioner's house, the soldiers pushing their bayonets, crying, make way! They took place by the custom house and, continuing to push to drive the people off, pricked some in several places, on which they were clamorous and, it is said, threw snow balls. On this, the Captain commanded them to fire; and more snow balls coming, he again said, damn you, fire, be the consequence what it will! One soldier then fired, and a townsman with a cudgel struck him over the hands with such force that he dropped his firelock; and, rushing forward, aimed a blow at the Captain's head which grazed his hat and fell pretty heavy upon his arm. However, the soldiers continued the fire successively till seven or eight or, as some say, eleven guns were discharged.

DOCUMENT 5

Source: John Andrews to William Barrell, Letter Regarding the Boston Tea Party (1773)

They muster'd I'm told, upon Fort Hill, to the number of about two hundred, and procceded, two by two, to Griffin's wharf, where Hall, Bruce, and Coffin lay, each with 114 chests of the ill fated article on board; the two former with only that article, but ye latter arriv'd at ye wharf only ye day before, was freighted with a large quantity of other goods, which they took the greatest care not to injure in the least, and before nine o'clock in ye evening, every chest from on board the three vessels was knock'd to pieces and flung over ye sides.

They say the actors were Indians from Narragansett. Whether they were or not, to a transient observer they appear'd as such, being cloath'd in Blankets with the heads muffled, and copper color'd countenances, being, each arm'd with a hatchet or axe, and pair pistols, nor was their dialect different from what I conceive these geniusses to speak, as their jargon was unintelligible to all but themselves. Not the least insult was offer'd to any person, save one Captain Conner, a letter of horses in this place, not many years since remov'd from dear Ireland, who had ript up the lining of his coat and waistcoat under the arms, and watch-ing, his opportunity had nearly fill'd them with tea, but being detected, was handled pretty roughly. They not only stripp'd him of his cloaths, but gave him a coat of mud, with a severe bruising into the bargain; and nothing but their utter aversion to make any disturbance pre-vented his being tar'd and feather'd.

DOCUMENT 6

Source: The Daughters of Liberty Urge Americans to Boycott British Goods.

Young ladies in town, and those that live round,
Let a friend at this season advise you:
Since money's so scarce, and times growing worse,
Strange things may soon hap and surprise you;
First then, throw aside your high top knots of pride,
Wear none but your own country linen,
Of Economy boast, let your pride be the most
To show clothes of your own make and spinning.

DOCUMENT 7

Source: James Otis, The Rights of the British Colonies Asserted and Proved (1763)

The form of government is by nature and by right so far left to the individuals of each society that they may alter it from a simple democracy or government of all over all to any other form they please. Such alteration may and ought to be made by express compact. But how seldom this right has been asserted, history will abundantly show. For once that it has been fairly settled by compact, fraud, force, or accident have determined it an hundred times. As the people have gained upon tyrants, these have been obliged to relax only till a fairer opportunity has put it in their power to encroach again...

     Now can there be any liberty where property is taken away without consent? Can it with any color of truth, justice, or equity be affirmed that the northern colonies are represented in Parliament? Has this whole continent of near three thousand miles in length, and in which and his other American dominions His Majesty has or very soon will have some millions of as good, loyal, and useful subjects, white and black, as any in the three king-doms, the election of one member of the House of Commons?

DOCUMENT 8

Source: The Crisis Comes to a Head: April 19, 1775

It is hoped however that this large Reinforcement to your Army will enable you to take a more active & determined part, & that you will have Strength enough, not only to keep Possession of Boston, but to give Protection in to Salem & the friends of Government at that Place, & that you may without Hazard of Insult return thither if you think fit, & exercise Your Functions there, conformable to His Majesty's Instructions.

     I have already said, in more Letters than one, that the Authority of this Kingdom must be supported, & the Execution of its Laws inforced, & you will have seen in His Maty's Speech to both Houses of Parliament, & in the Addresses which they have presented to His Majesty, the firm Resolution of His Majesty and Parliament to act upon those Principles; and as there is a strong Appearance that the Body of the People in at least three of the New England Governments are determined to cast off their Dependence upon the Government of this Kingdom, the only Consideration that remains is, in what manner the Force under your Command may be exerted to defend the Constitution & to restore the Vigour of Government.

DOCUMENT 9

Source: A Freelance Writer Urges His Readers To Use Common Sense (1776)

To the evil of monarchy we have added that of hereditary succession; and as the first is a degradation and lessening of ourselves, so the second, claimed as a matter of right, is an insult and an imposition on posterity. For all men being originally equals, no one by birth could have a right to set up his own family in perpetual preference to all others for ever, and though himself might deserve some decent degree of honors of his contemporaries, yet his descendants might be far too unworthy to inherit them. One of the strongest natural proofs of the folly of hereditary right in kings, is, that nature disapproves it, otherwise she would not so frequently turn it into ridicule by giving mankind an ass for a lion. Secondly, as no man at first could possess any other public honors than were bestowed upon him, so the givers of those honors could have no power to give away the right of posterity, and though they might say 'We choose you for our head,' they could not, without manifest injustice to their children, say 'that your children and your children's children shall reign over ours for ever.' Because such an unwise, unjust, unnatural compact might (perhaps) in the next succession put them under the government of a rogue or a fool. Most wise men, in their private sentiments, have ever treated hereditary right with contempt; yet it is one of those evils, which when once established is not easily removed; many submit from fear, others from superstition, and the more powerful part shares with the king the plunder of the rest.

DOCUMENT 10

Source: Thomas Jefferson, "Original Rough Draught" of the Declaration of Independence (1776)

We hold these truths to be sacred & undeniable that all men are created equal & independant, that from that equal creation they derive rights inherent & inalienable, among which are the preservation of life, & liberty, & the pursuit of happiness; that to secure these ends, governments are instituted among men, deriving their just powers from the consent of the governed; that whenever any form of government shall become destructive of these ends, it is the right of the people to alter or to abolish it, & to institute new government, laying its foundation on such principles & organising it's powers in such form, as to them shall seem most likely to effect their safety & happiness.

7. THE AMERICAN REVOLUTION, 1776–1786

CHAPTER OVERVIEW

Summary

Victory in the American Revolution came neither swiftly nor easily for the American Patriots. The colonies were racked with divisions as evidenced by the significant number of Loyalists who supported the British. Patriots, also, were confronted by a tremendous military power that could offer Indians and enslaved African Americans greener pastures, thereby attracting many of them to their side. Furthermore, the young nation struggled to find an acceptable mode of governance which confounded efforts to fund and supply the military with what it needed to win. However, this scarcity of advantages bound the faithful together in a new national community, which in the end proved sufficient to secure victory. Through the determined leadership of men like George Washington, the Continental Army was successful enough to convince France, the Dutch, and Spain to directly or indirectly support the United States with men, material, and money. This combination of will and willing allies ultimately wore the British down and yielded American independence. Having achieved its independence, the United States soon faced new challenges as the postwar economy took a downturn and a growing debate over the meaning of freedom led many to press state and national governments for new and unprecedented changes.

Focus Questions

1. What were the major alignments and divisions among Americans during the American Revolution?

2. What were the major campaigns of the Revolution?

3. What role did the Articles of Confederation and the Confederation Congress play in the Revolution?

4. In what ways were the states the sites for significant political change?

CHAPTER REVIEW

Short Response: Consider these questions thoughtfully. Respond with the best possible short answer by filling in the blank.

1. The hardship suffered by George Washington's soldiers during the winter camp at _____ eventually became a symbol American nationalism.

2. During the American Revolution, the _____ was a much more important fighting force than the state militias in achieving independence.

3. _____ were American colonists who supported the British during the Revolution.

4. _____ was a hero of the early battles of the Revolution on the Patriot side, but in 1779, resentful of what he perceived to be humiliating assignments and rank below his station, he became a paid informer of the British.

5. _____ was a notable woman activist who turned her home into a center of Patriot political activity and published a series of satires supporting the American cause and scorning the Loyalists.

6. On Christmas night 1776, George Washington led 2,400 troops across the _____ and the next morning defeated the Hessian forces in a surprise attack.

7. British general John Burgoyne was surrounded and surrendered his forces on October 19, 1777 at

_____.

8. General Cornwallis surrendered a major British Army in 1781 following the siege of

_____.

9. _____ is the American artist who painted "Surrender of Lord Cornwallis."

10. The ratification of the _____ in 1781 created the first national government of the United States.

Multiple Choice: Select the response that best answers each question or best completes each sentence.

1. The overall casualty rate during the Revolution:
    a. was greater than all other US conflicts except the Civil War.
    b. was low because of the primitive weapons used.
    c. dropped considerably after the bloodshed of Bunker's Hill.
    d. is entirely unknown because of poor record keeping.

2. Many of those who remained loyal to Britain:
    a. were recent immigrants.
    b. held royal offices within the colonies.
    c. were ethnic minorities who had faced persecution or harassment in the colonies.
    d. All of the Above.

3. The largest number of Loyalists who left the United States during the Revolution:
    a. traveled to England.
    b. joined the British Army.
    c. moved to Canada.
    d. migrated to the Caribbean.

4. The first nation to sign a formal treaty of alliance with the United States was:
    a. Belgium.
    b. France.
    c. Holland.
    d. Ireland.

5. During the American Revolution:
    a. of the Indian tribes that became involved, the majority supported Great Britain.
    b. Indians supported the French position and eagerly sided with the United States.
    c. about half the tribes fought for the British and about half supported the United States.
    d. Indians saw the conflict as a "white-man's war," and none of the tribes became involved.

6. The war in the South was characterized by:
    a. British capture of major port cities.
    b. vicious violence between Patriots and Loyalists.
    c. very little serious fighting.

d. large scale Patriot recruiting of Southern slaves for military service.

7. Patriot victory at Yorktown resulted from:
    a. the successful joint efforts of American and French forces.
    b. Washington's clever, silent assault across the Hudson River.
    c. the last minute discovery of Benedict Arnold's treachery.
    d. discovered plans taken from Major Andre.

8. The Articles of Confederation:
    a. created a powerful central government with full authority to sustain and support the war effort.
    b. established a relatively weak central government that faced numerous challenges during the war.
    c. were a plan of government that the states used as a model when they wrote their own constitutions.
    d. proved so inadequate that in 1780, Congress replaced them with the Constitution of the United States.

9. A serious impediment to the ratification of the Articles of Confederation was:
    a. Rhode Island's demand for a stronger executive branch.
    b. what to do with Indian claims for land east of the Mississippi River.
    c. the decision to wait and see if Canada would join the union as well.
    d. the lingering dispute over state claims to western lands.

10. Under the terms of the Treaty of Paris of 1783:
    a. the United States pledged to treat Loyalists fairly.
    b. the United States gained all English territory east of the Mississippi River except Florida and Canada .
    c. the British retained complete control of the Mississippi but not St. Lawrence River.
    d. A & B.

11. The Northwest Ordinance of 1787:
    a. prohibited slavery in the newly won territories north of the Ohio River.
    b. demanded that the British leave its posts on the western frontier immediately.
    c. recognized Spanish claims in the trans-Mississippi region and prohibited all American settlement there.
    d. made peace with Indians who had allied with the British in the Revolution.

12. The Virginia Declaration of Rights that became a precedent for the Bill of Rights were written by:
    a. Thomas Jefferson.
    b. Winthrop Jordan.
    c. George Mason.
    d. John Adams.

13. In the aftermath of the Revolution:
    a. some Americans hoped that political changes would lead to other reforms.
    b. American women were given the right to vote for the first time in history.
    c. Thomas Jefferson advocated policies of primogeniture and entail in Virginia.
    d. most Americans hoped to see an established church in the United States.

14. Thomas Jefferson's Bill for Establishing Religious Freedom:
    a. declared that the United States was a Christian nation.
    b. ended the Anglican Church's position as the official, tax supported church of Virginia.
    c. marked the end of all religious tests for officeholders in the United States
    d. was defeated by the legislature for being too tolerant toward Catholics.

15. During and in the years following the Revolution:
    a. thousands of African Americans who fought with the British were forced to flee the country.

b. Pennsylvania, Connecticut, and Rhode Island passed gradual emancipation laws.
c. the free black population of Virginia grew to more than 20,000.
d. all of the above.

Thought Questions: Think carefully about the following questions or comments. Your answers should prepare you to participate in class discussions or help you to write an effective essay. In both class discussions and essays you should always support the arguments you make by referring to specific examples and historical evidence. You may use the space provided to sketch out ideas or outline your response.

1. What were the major problems that plagued the Patriots during the American Revolution? What advantages did the Patriots possess?

2. Discuss the role of the United States' ally France and other major powers that helped influence the outcome of the American Revolution. What assistance, if any, did the United States receive from other global powers?

3. Discuss the Articles of Confederation. Why did the Americans seek to create a government of this form? What were the difficulties that this new government faced because of its structure?

4.   The American Revolution brought about great changes from the old colonial order. What were some of the most important changes brought about by the Revolution? What were some of the reforms that many began to expect or demand in the wake of victory in the Revolution?

Map Skills: These questions are based on the maps in the chapter. Please use the blank map provided here for your answers.

1. Indicate the following sites of significant events during the American Revolution: Trenton, Princeton, Valley Forge, Cowpens, Guilford Courthouse, and Yorktown.

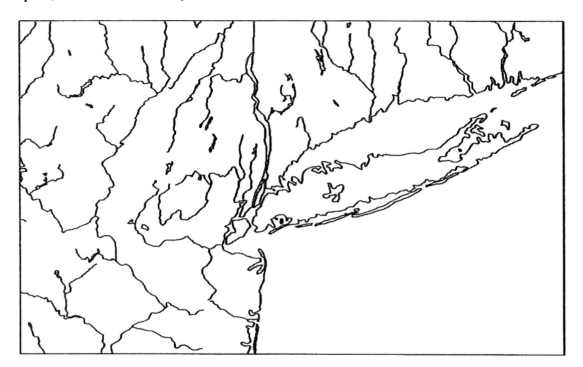

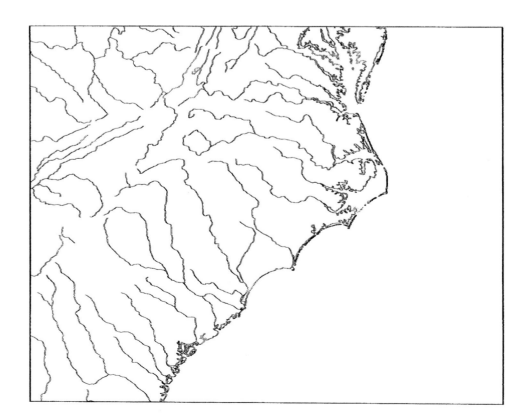

2. Use the map to locate the borders of the United States in 1783, the areas in dispute with England, the area jointly claimed by the United States and Spain, as well as Spanish Louisiana, and Texas.

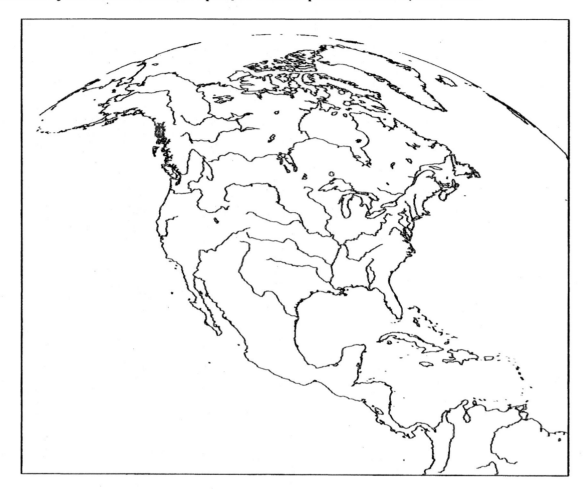

3. Indicate the Northwest Territory boundary and identify each of the Great Lakes. Identify the political boundaries of the five states created out of the territory.

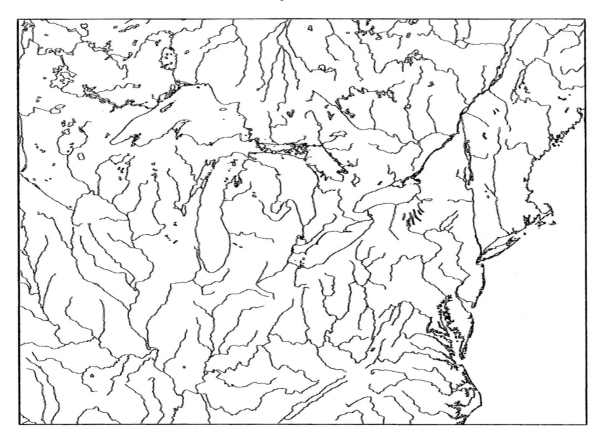

Interpreting the Past

Name _____Date _____

**What goals did the colonists have in waging the Revolutionary War
and how did these goals shape their emergent political system?**

DOCUMENT 1

A Freelance Writer Urges His Readers to Use Common Sense (1776)
Source: A Hypertext on American History From the Colonial Period Until Modern Times,
http://odur.let.rug.nl/~usa/D/1776-1800/paine/CM/sense03.htm

The nearer any government approaches to a republic the less business there is for a king. It is somewhat difficult to find a proper name for the government of England. Sir William Meredith calls it a republic; but in its present state it is unworthy of the name, because the corrupt influence If the crown, by having all the places in its disposal, hath so effectually swallowed up the power, and eaten out the virtue of the house of commons (the republican part in the constitution) that the government of England is nearly as monarchical as that of France or Spain. Men fall out with names without understanding them. For it is the republican and not the monarchical part of the constitution of England which Englishmen glory in, viz. the liberty of choosing an house of commons from out of their own body and it is easy to see that when the republican virtue fails, slavery ensues. My is the constitution of England sickly, but because monarchy hath poisoned the republic, the crown hath engrossed the commons?

DOCUMENT 2

Source: Thomas Jefferson, "Original Rough Draught" of the Declaration of Independence (1776)

We therefore the representatives of the United States of America in General Congress assembled do, in the name & by authority of the good people of these states, reject and renounce all allegiance & subject to the kings of Great Britain & all others who may hereafter claim by, through, or under them; we utterly dissolve & break off all political connection which may have heretofore subsisted between us & the people or parliament of Great Britain; and finally we do assert and declare these colonies to be free and independent states, and that as free & independent states they shall hereafter have power to levy war, conclude peace, contract alliances, establish commerce, & to do all other acts and things which independent states may of right do. And for the support of this declaration we mutually pledge to each other our lives, our fortunes, & our sacred honour.

DOCUMENT 3

The TORY'S Day of JUDGMENT.

DOCUMENT 4

Source: Rights of Women in an Independent Republic

Abigail Adams to John Adams, Braintree, 31 March 1776

I long to hear that you have declared an independency-and by the way in the new Code of Laws which I suppose it will be necessary for you to make I desire you would Remember the Ladies, and be more generous and favourable to them than your ancestors. Do not put such unlimited power into the hands of the Husbands. Remember all Men would be tyrants if they could. If particular care and attention is not paid to the Ladies we are determined to foment a Rebellion, and will not hold ourselves bound by any Laws in which we have no voice, or Representation.

That your Sex are Naturally Tyrannical is a Truth so thoroughly established as to admit of no dispute, but such of you as wish to be happy willingly give up the harsh title of Master for the more tender and endearing one of Friend. Why then, not put it out of the power of the vicious and the Lawless to use us with cruelty and indignity with impunity. Men of Sense in all Ages abhor those customs which treat us only as the vassals of your Sex. Regard us then as Beings placed by providence under your protection and in imitation of the Supreme Being make use of that power only for our happiness.

DOCUMENT 5

Source: African Americans and the Revolution

In this excerpt, Cato and his family, slaves freed because their owner failed to comply with slave registration laws, wrote the following to the legislature to uphold the law and their freedom:

We esteem in a particular blessing granted to us, that we are enabled this day to add one more step to universal civilization by removing as much as possible the sorrows of those who have lived in "undeserved" bondage, and from which by the assumed authority of the kings of Great Britain, no effectual legal relief could be obtained.

Extending his writing to a political scene, in this excerpt Benjamin Banneker addresses Thomas Jefferson regarding slavery:

Sir, Suffer me to recall to your mind that time in which the Arms and tyranny of the British Crown were exerted with powerful effort, in order to reduce you to a State of Servitude . . . You cannot but acknowledge, that the present freedom and tranquility which you enjoy you have mercifully received, and that is the peculiar blessing of Heaven.

DOCUMENT 6

Source: Constitution of Pennsylvania (1776)

A Declaration of the Rights of the Inhabitants of the Commonwealth, or State of Pennsylvania

I. That all men are born equally free and independent, and have certain natural inherent and inalienable rights, amongst which are the enjoying and defending life and liberty, acquiring, possessing and protecting property, and pursuing and obtaining happiness and safety.

II. That all men have a natural and unalienable right to worship Almighty God according to the dictates of their own consciences and understanding: And that no man ought or of right can be compelled to attend any religious worship, or erect or support any place of worship, or maintain any ministry, contrary to, or against, his own free will and consent: Nor can any man, who acknowledges the being of a God, be justly deprived or abridged of any civil right as a citizen, on account of his religious sentiments or peculiar mode of religious worship: And that no authority can or ought to be vested in, or assumed by any power whatever, that shall in any case interfere with, or in any manner controul, the right of conscience in the free exercise of religious worship.

III. That the people of this State have the sole, exclusive and inherent right of governing and regulating the internal police of the same.

IV. That all power being originally inherent in, and consequently derived from, the people; therefore all officers of government, whether legislative or executive, are their trustees and servants, and at all times accountable to them.

V. That government is, or ought to be, instituted for the common benefit, protection and security of the people, nation or community; and not for the particular emolument or advantage of any single man, family or set of men, who are a part only of that community; And that the community hath an indubitable, unalienable and indefeasible right to reform, alter, or abolish government in such a manner as shall be by that community judged most conducive to the public weal.

VI. That those who are employed in the legislative and executive business of the State, may be restrained from oppression, the people have a right, at such periods as they may think proper, to reduce their public officers to a private station, and supply the vacancies by certain and regular elections.

VII. That all elections ought to be free; and that all free men having a sufficient evident common interest with, and attachment to the community, have a right to elect officers, or to be elected into office.

DOCUMENT 7

A Declaration of the Rights of the Inhabitants of the Commonwealth of Massachusetts (1780)
Source: Francis N. Thorpe, ed., The Federal and State Constitutions, 7 vols. (Washington, D.C., Government Printing Office, 1909), vol. III, pp. 1888–1895.

ARTICLE IV. The people of this commonwealth have the sole and exclusive right of governing themselves, as a free, sovereign, and independent state; and do, and forever hereafter shall, exercise and enjoy every power, jurisdiction, and right, which is not, or may not hereafter be, by them expressly delegated to the United States of America, in Congress assembled.

ARTICLE V. All power residing originally in the people, and being derived from them, the several magistrates and officers of government, vested with authority, whether legislative, executive, or judicial, are their substitutes and agents, and are at all times accountable to them.

ARTICLE VI. No man, nor corporation, or association of men, have any other title to obtain advantages, or particular and exclusive privileges, distinct from those of the community, than what arises from the consideration of services rendered to the public; and this title being in nature neither hereditary, nor transmissible to children, or descendants, or relations by blood, the idea of a man born a magistrate, lawgiver, or judge, is absurd and unnatural.

ARTICLE VII. Government is instituted for the common good; for the protection, safety, prosperity, and happiness of the people; and not for the profit, honor, or private interest of any one man, family, or class of men: Therefore the people alone have an incontestable unalienable, and indefeasible right to institute government; and to reform, alter, or totally change the same, when their protection, safety, prosperity, and happiness require it.

ARTICLE VIII. In order to prevent those who are vested with authority from becoming oppressors, the people have a right at such periods and in such manner as they shall establish by their frame of government, to cause their public officers to return to private life; and to fill up vacant places by certain and regular elections and appointments.

ARTICLE IX. All elections ought to be free; and all the inhabitants of this commonwealth having such qualifications as they shall establish by their frame of government, have an equal right to elect officers, and to be elected, for public employments.

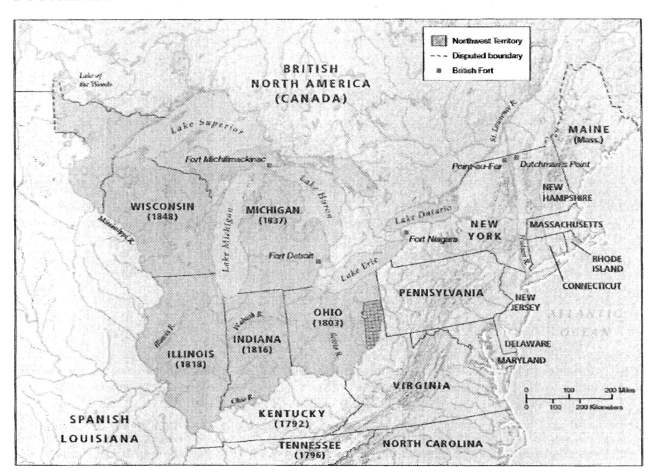

8. THE NEW NATION, 1786–1800

CHAPTER OVERVIEW

Summary

During the first decade and a half after the American Revolution, the young United States faced significant internal and external challenges. The domestic economy soured in the first few years after the war ended, and many communities faced hardship and revolt as a result. To the South and West, the Spanish and Indian peoples challenged the United States' claim to territories provided to it under the terms of the Treaty of Paris. Internal debates over the need for a new constitution divided the nation along regional and ideological lines. Once unified in their opposition to the British, many in the founding generation now found themselves embroiled in heated political disputes as members of rival parties. Yet through it all, Americans of many stripes were part of an emergent national identity that drew strength from a vibrant and increasingly democratic political life.

Focus Questions

1. What were the tensions and conflicts between local and national authorities in the decades after the American Revolution?

2. How did Americans differ in their views of the new Constitution, and how were those differences reflected in the struggle to achieve ratification?

3. What were the essential structures of national government under the Constitution?

4. How did American political parties first begin?

5. What were the first stirrings of an authentic American national culture?

CHAPTER REVIEW

Short Response: Consider these questions thoughtfully. Respond with the best possible short answer by filling in the blank.

1. The tax revolt in Massachusetts in 1786 is known as _____ .

2. The Constitutional Convention was held in _____ in 1787.

3. At the Constitutional Convention, the _____ was a proposal to scrap the Articles of Confederation in favor of a "consolidated government" with the power to tax and to enforce its laws directly rather than through the states.

4. The word _____ appeared nowhere in the Constitution yet Southern interests were protected in the final version of the Constitution.

5. Those who opposed ratifying the Constitution were known as the _____.

6. Those who supported ratifying the Constitution were known as the _____.

7. The series of essays written by Hamilton, Madison, and Jay in support of the Constitution are known as
_____.

8. In 1790, _____ became the last of the original colonies to ratify the Constitution.

9. The first ten amendments to the Constitution are known as the _____.

10. During the _____ President Washington sent 13,000 soldiers to Western Pennsylvania.

Multiple Choice: Select the response that best answers each question or best completes each sentence.

1. The most important result of Shays' Rebellion was:
    a. that it guaranteed the independence of the United States of America.
    b. the response by Americans who wanted a stronger national government.
    c. the creation of Maine as a state out of territory claimed by Massachusetts.
    d. the confirmation that the national government could ensure law and order.

2. In the years just after the Revolution:
    a. American manufacturers drove British products out of the US market.
    b. the national currency enjoyed a significant increase in value.
    c. the US economy slipped into a significant depression.
    d. the British cut off al trade with the United States.

3. The men who attended the Constitutional Convention:
    a. were committed to creating a democratic form of government.
    b. regretted leaving the protective hand of Britain.
    c. represented twelve of the nation's thirteen states.
    d. were mostly small farmers and craftsmen by trade.

4. Much of what we know about the Constitutional Convention is because of the voluminous notes taken by:
    a. James K. Polk.
    b. Patrick Henry.
    c. John Locke.
    d. James Madison.

5. Opposition to the new Constitution:
    a. came mostly from those who felt the Articles of Confederation were inadequate.
    b. grew in part out of fears of a strong national government.
    c. was almost non-existent.
    d. faded after Rhode Island became the first state to ratify it.

6. An important goal of Alexander Hamilton was to:
    a. get the government to repudiate the states' and the nation's debt from the Revolution.
    b. establish the good credit of the new nation and to protect American manufacturers.
    c. acquire new territory to be the foundation to create an agrarian empire for liberty.
    d. make sure that John Adams was elected president once Washington left office.

7. Which of the following is not included in the Bill of Rights:
    a. freedom of speech.
    b. the right of petition.
    c. the right to vote.
    d. the prohibition of double jeopardy.

8. By agreeing to accept Hamilton's plan for the federal government to assume state debts:
    a. Congress doomed the US to a decade of economic hardship.
    b. foreign and domestic creditors lost millions of dollars.
    c. Southerners were rewarded by having the nation's capitol situated along the Potomac River.
    d. Thomas Jefferson was voted out of office.

9. The French Revolution:
    a. exacerbated the deep split between the Federalists and the Republicans.
    b. was largely ignored by the people of the US.
    c. helped trigger the American Revolution.
    d. forced George Washington to send troops to France.

10. American farmers and merchants gained access to the port of New Orleans from Spain:
    a. by Jay's Treaty.
    b. when the United States invaded Louisiana in 1794.
    c. by Pinckney's Treaty.
    d. only after the Spanish abandoned the province.

11. The XYZ Affair involved diplomatic relations between the United States and:
    a. England.
    b. France.
    c. Germany.
    d. Russia.

12. One result of the peaceful transfer of power in 1800 was:
    a. an expansion in the popular interest in politics.
    b. the end of the Federalists as a viable political party.
    c. the creation of the Democratic Party in the United States.
    d. a general decline in people joining political parties.

13. Jeffersonian Republicans played an important role in establishing a free press in the United States by:
    a. establishing the first partisan newspaper.

b. their actions in opposing the Sedition Act.
c. passing the First Amendment to the Constitution.
d. creating the position of White House Press Secretary.

14. The second President of the United States was:
   a. Thomas Jefferson.
   b. John Adams.
   c. Alexander Hamilton.
   d. James Madison.

15. The Revolution of 1800:
   a. refers to the first time the Federalists won a presidential election.
   b. led to the ratification of the twelfth amendment to the US Constitution.
   c. was prevented by sending soldiers to Western Pennsylvania.
   d. led to the expansion of the United States Army.

Thought Questions: Think carefully about the following questions or comments. Your answers should prepare you to participate in class discussions or help you to write an effective essay. In both class discussions and essays you should always support the arguments you make by referring to specific examples and historical evidence. You may use the space provided to sketch out ideas or outline your response.

1. What were some of the major challenges facing the United States after the American Revolution? How and why did Shays' Rebellion cause such concern among many prominent Americans?

2. Outline and describe the major arguments that Federalists used to defend ratifying the Constitution. Why did the Anti-Federalists oppose ratification? Where was opposition to and support for the Constitution strongest?

3. In what ways did the Federalists and the Republicans differ? How were these differences reflected in the policies they supported and/or opposed?

4. What were the principle foreign policy challenges and achievements of the United States during the presidencies of Washington and Adams?

Map Skills: These questions are based on the maps in the chapter. Please use the blank map provided here for your answers.

1. Locate those areas of the United States where support for the Constitution was strong, where the opposition was strongest, and where opinions were fairly evenly split.

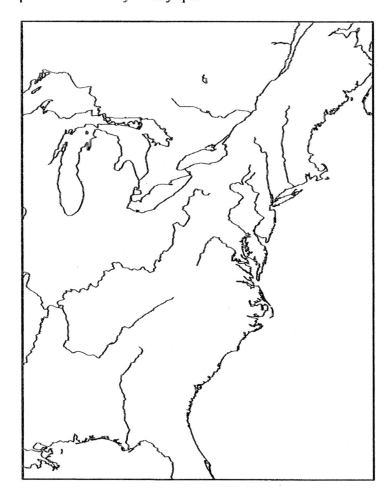

2. Identify the boundaries of the United States and land claimed by Spain on the map below. Identify where the claims of these two nation's overlapped. Also, identify the Mississippi River and the City of New Orleans.

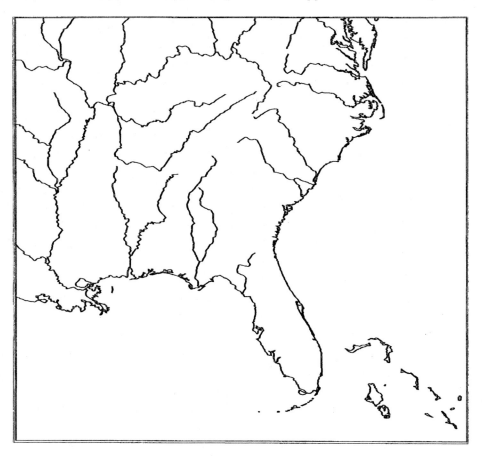

3. Use the map to indicate the parts of the United States that supported the Federalists and those that voted Democratic-Republican in the election of 1800.

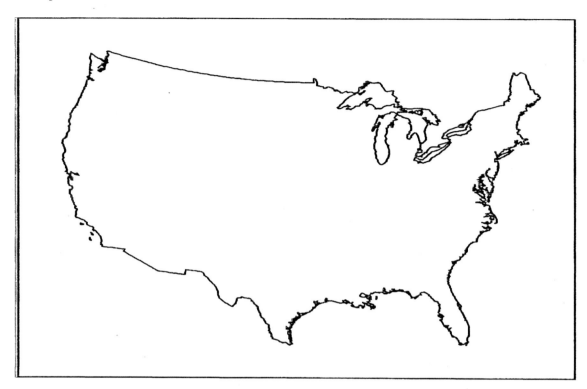

Interpreting the Past

Name _____ Date _____

What were some of the issues involved in the debate surrounding the composition and ratification of the Constitution?

DOCUMENT 1

Source: Constitution of Pennsylvania (1776)

I. That all men are born equally free and independent, and have certain natural inherent and inalienable rights, amongst which are the enjoying and defending life and liberty, acquiring, possessing and protecting property, and pursuing and obtaining happiness and safety.

II. That all men have a natural and unalienable right to worship Almighty God according to the dictates of their own consciences and understanding: And that no man ought or of right can be compelled to attend any religious worship, or erect or support any place of worship, or maintain any ministry, contrary to, or against, his own free will and consent: Nor can any man, who acknowledges the being of a God, be justly deprived or abridged of any civil right as a citizen, on account of his religious sentiments or peculiar mode of religious worship: And that no authority can or ought to be vested in, or assumed by any power whatever, that shall in any case interfere with, or in any manner controul, the right of consciencein the free exercise of religious worship...

XI. That in controversies respecting property, and in suits between man and man, the parties have a right to trial by jury, which ought to be held sacred.

XII. That the people have a right to freedom of speech, and of writing, and publishing their sentiments; therefore the freedom of the press ought not to be restrained.

XIII. That the people have a right to bear arms for the defence of themselves and the state; and as standing armies in the time of peace are dangerous to liberty, they ought not to be kept up; And that the military should be kept under strict subordination to, and governed by, the civil power.

DOCUMENT 2

Source: A Declaration of the Rights of the Inhabitants of the Commonwealth of Massachusetts (1780)

CHAPTER I
THE LEGISLATIVE POWER SECTION I. THE GENERAL COURT
ARTICLE I. The department of legislation shall be formed by two branches, a Senate and House of Representatives; each of which shall have a negative on the other.
The legislative body shall assemble every year [on the last Wednesday in May, and at such other times as they shall judge necessary; and shall dissolve and be dissolved on the day next preceding the said last Wednesday in May;] and shall be styled, THE GENERAL COURT OF MASSACHUSETTS.

DOCUMENT 3

Source: Henry Knox, Letter to George Washington (1786)

Our political machine, composed of thirteen independent sovereignties, have been perpetually operating against each other and against the federal head ever since the peace. The powers of Congress are totally inadequate to preserve the balance between the respective States, and oblige them to do those things which are essential for their own welfare or for the general good. The frame of mind in the local legislatures seems to be exerted to prevent the federal constitution from having any good effect. The machine works inversely to the public good in all its parts: not only is State against State, and all against the federal head, but the States within themselves possess the name only without having the essential concomitant of government, the power of preserving the peace, the protection of the liberty and property of the citizens. On the very first impression of faction and licentiousness, the fine theoretic government of Massachusetts has given way, and its laws [are] trampled under foot. Men at a distance, who have admired our systems of government unfounded in nature, are apt to accuse the rulers, and say that taxes have been assessed too high and collected too rigidly. This is a deception equal to any that has been hitherto entertained. That taxes may be the ostensible cause is true, but that they are the true cause is as far remote from truth as light from darkness. The people who are the insurgents have never paid any or but very little taxes. But they see the weakness of government: they feel at once their own poverty compared with the opulent, and their own force, and they are determined to make use of the latter in order to remedy the former.

DOCUMENT 4

Source: Marquis de Chastellux, Travels in North America (1786)

The government [of Virginia] may become democratic, as it is at the present moment; but the national character, the very spirit of the government, will always be aristocratic. Nor can this be doubted when one considers that another cause is still operating to produce the same result. I am referring to slavery, not because it is a mark of distinction or special privilege to possess Negroes, but because the sway held over them nourishes vanity and sloth, two vices which accord wonderfully with established prejudices. It will doubtless be asked how these prejudices have been reconciled with the present revolution, founded on such different principles. I shall answer that they have perhaps contributed to it; that while New England revolted through reason and calculation, Virginia revolted through pride. . . .

DOCUMENT 5

Source: Thomas Jefferson to James Madison

Paris, January 30th, 1787
Dear Sir,
…Societies exist under three forms, sufficiently distinguishable: (1) without government, as among our Indians; (2) under governments, wherein the will of everyone has a just influence, as is the case in England, in a slight degree, and in our states, in a great one; (3) under governments of force, as is the case in all other monarchies, and in most of the other republics.

To have an idea of the curse of existence under these last, they must be seen. It is a government of wolves over sheep. It is a problem, not clear in my mind, that the first condition is not the best. But I believe it to be inconsistent with any great degree of population. The second state has a great deal of good in it. The mass of mankind under that enjoys a precious degree of liberty and happiness. It has its evils, too, the principal of which is the turbulence to which it is subject. But weigh this against the oppressions of monarchy, and it becomes nothing. *Malo periculosam libertatem quam quietam servitutem.* Even this evil is productive of good. It prevents the degeneracy of government and nourishes a general attention to the public affairs.
I hold it that a little rebellion now and then is a good thing, and as necessary in the political world as storms in the physical. Unsuccessful rebellions, indeed, generally establish the encroachments on the rights of the people which have produced them. An observation of this truth should render honest republican governors so mild in their punishment of rebellions as not to discourage them too much. It is a medicine necessary for the sound health of government. . . .
Yours affectionately,
Th. Jefferson

DOCUMENT 6

The "Distracting Question" in Philadelphia (1787)
Source: The Avalon Project at the Yale Law School http://www.yale.edu/lawweb/avalon/debates/711.htm

Wednesday July 11, 1787
IN CONVENTION
...Mr. WILLIAMSON was for making it the duty of the Legislature to do what was right & not leaving it at liberty to do or not do it. He moved that Mr. Randolph's proposition be postponed. in order to consider the following "that in order to ascertain the alterations that may happen in the population & wealth of the several States, a census shall be taken of the free white inhabitants and 3/5 ths. of those of other descriptions on the 1st. year after this Government shall have been adopted and every year thereafter; and that the Representation be regulated accordingly."

DOCUMENT 7

Patrick Henry Speaks Against Ratification of the Constitution (1788)
Source: Jonathan Elliot, ed., The Debates in the Several State Conventions on the Adoption of the Federal Constitution 2nd ed., 5 vols. (Philadelphia: J. B. Lippincott Company, 1907).

...And here I would make this inquiry of those worthy characters who composed a part of the late federal Convention. I am sure they were fully impressed with the necessity of forming a great consolidated government, instead of a confederation. That this is a consolidated government is demonstrably clear; and the danger of such a government is, to my mind, very striking I have the highest veneration for those gentlemen; but, sir, give me leave to demand, What right had they to say, We, the people? My political curiosity, exclusive of my anxious solicitude for the public welfare, leads me to ask, Who authorized them to speak the language of, We, the people,instead of, We, the states? States are the characteristics and the soul of a confederation. If the states be not the agents of this compact, it must be one great, consolidated, national government, of the people of all the states. . .. It is not mere curiosity that actuates me: I wish to hear the real, actual, existing danger, which should lead us to take those steps, so dangerous in my conception.

DOCUMENT 8

James Madison Defends the Constitution (1788)
Source: Jonathan Elliot, ed., The Debates in the Several State Conventions on the Adoption of the Federal Constitution. 2nd ed., 5 vols. (Philadelphia: J. B. Lippincott Company, 1907).

...Give me leave to say something of the nature of the government, and to show that it is safe and just to vest it with the power of taxation. There are a number of opinions; but the principal question is, whether it be a federal or consolidated government. In order to judge properly of the question before us, we must consider it minutely in its principal parts. I conceive myself that it is of a mixed nature; it is in a manner unprecedented; we cannot find one express example in the experience of the world. It stands by itself. In some respects it is a government of a federal nature; in others, it is of a consolidated nature. Even if we attend to the manner in which the Constitution is investigated, ratified, and made the act of the people of America, I can say, notwithstanding what the honorable gentleman has alleged, that this government is not completely consolidated, nor is it entirely federal. Who are parties to it? The people but not the people as composing one great body; but the people as composing thirteen sovereignties. Were it, as the gentleman asserts, a consolidated government, the assent of a majority of the people would be sufficient for its establishment; and, as a majority have adopted it already, the remaining states would be bound by the act of the majority, even if they unanimously reprobated it. Were it such a government as is suggested, it would be now binding on the people of this state, without having had the privilege of deliberating upon it. But, sir, no state is bound by it, as it is, without its own consent. Should all the states adopt it, it will be then a government established by the thirteen states of America, not through the intervention of the legislatures, but by the people at large. In this particular respect, the distinction between the existing and proposed governments is very material. The existing system has been derived from the dependent derivative authority of the legislatures of the states; whereas this is derived from the superior power of the people.

9. AN EMPIRE FOR LIBERTY, 1790–1824

CHAPTER OVERVIEW

Summary

During the late eighteenth and early nineteenth centuries, the United States was part of a continuing contest to occupy and control territory in North America. The United States proved quite successful in this competition as its territory roughly doubled as a result of victory in Indian wars and a fortuitous purchase. This success came despite the ambitions and wishes of the British, Spanish, Russian, and Indian peoples. As its territory grew the American people pushed ever westward in a trek for greener pastures. Leaders like Thomas Jefferson endorsed this mobility and smiled at the prospect that democracy and virtuous farmers might overstretch the continent. However, this optimism would be tested by a new conflict with an old enemy and internal debates over just what kind of democracy ought to follow in the wake of expansion.

Focus Questions

1. Where did the new nation find economic opportunities in the world market?

2. How did Jefferson's presidency calm the political differences of the 1790s?

3. What values were embodied in republican agrarianism?

4. What unresolved issues between the United States and Britain led to the War of 1812?

5. What were the causes of Indian resistance, and how did the War of 1812 resolve them?

6. How did the Missouri Compromise reveal the dangers of expansion?

CHAPTER REVIEW

Short Response: Consider these questions thoughtfully. Respond with the best possible short answer by filling in the blank.

1. _____ was the fifteen-year-old Lemhi woman, who became the only female to join Lewis and Clark on their westward journey.

2. Lewis and Clark ultimately reached the Pacific Ocean at the mouth of the _____ River.

3. In 1800 the nation's largest city was _____ with a population of approximately 70,000.

4. The United States faced a new North American competitor as the _____ expanded fur trading settlements in what is today Alaska.

5. _____became North America's first independent black nation after a successful slave revolt in 1791.

6. During the 1790s _____ and _____ became the United States' first Trans-Appalachian states.

7. The 1793 invention of the _____ transformed the South's staple cash crop economy.

8. The presidencies of Thomas Jefferson, James Madison and James Monore became known as the

_____.

9. _____ published his deeply pessimistic and widely influential *Essay on the Principle of Population* in 1798.

10. Under _____ direction, the Supreme Court became a powerful nationalizing force, often to the dismay of defenders of states' rights.

Multiple Choice: Select the response that best answers each question or best completes each sentence.

1. Each of the following were major Americans cities in 1800 except:
    a. Charleston.
    b. Baltimore.
    c. Philadelphia.
    d. Washington, D.C.

2. The leader of the successful slave revolt in the French colony of Saint Domingue was:
    a. Marquis de Lafayette.
    b. Toussaint L'Ouverture
    c. Francois DeGaulle.
    d. Pierre L'Enfant.

3. During the early nineteenth century:
   a. the American population was largely sedentary because of fears of frontier violence.
   b. migration became a common feature of American life.
   c. the US population fell slightly to less than 3 million people.
   d. the US population was predominately urban.

4. The inauguration of President Thomas Jefferson was a significant occasion because:
   a. he was the first president to be elected by popular vote of the American people.
   b. it marked the peaceful transition of power from one political party to another.
   c. it was such a complete and radical break with the previous administrations.
   d. he initiated the era in American history known as Radical Republicanism.

5. The Chief Justice of the Supreme Court who in 1803 wrote the landmark decision in Marbury v. Madison was:
   a. Samuel Chase.
   b. John Jay.
   c. John Marshall.
   d. Earl Warren.

6. Thomas Jefferson believed:
   a. that the expansion of the nation was essential to liberty.
   b. all people should be free and equal in the United States.
   c. that Indians were not welcome in any part of the nation.
   d. slavery should not be allowed to expand into Louisiana.

7. In contrast to Washington and Adams, Jefferson:
   a. sought to restore near monarchical style to the office of President.
   b. tried to end slavery in the nation's capitol.
   c. abandoned the Republican Party to become a Federalist.
   d. rejected the high styled symbolism of the preceding two administrations.

8. The policies behind the ideal of republican agrarianism:
   a. centered on the need to increase manufacturing throughout the nation.
   b. limited the spread of slavery.
   c. rested on the idea that "those who labor in the earth are the chosen people of God."
   d. tried to protect the central features of Hamilton's economic program.

9. The United States acquired the Louisiana territory:
   a. from the Spanish in exchange for a pledge not to seize Florida.
   b. for a paltry $15 million.
   c. by cutting off all access to the Mississippi River.
   d. because Napoleon feared American military might.

10. The new generation of politicians who openly resisted British influence in North America was called:
    a. America Firsters.
    b. Isolationists.
    c. Patriots.
    d. War Hawks.

11. The Hartford Convention:
    a. strongly expressed New England Federalists' opposition to the War of 1812.
    b. concluded the peace treaty that ended the war with England late in 1814.
    c. was the first national meeting to nominate a presidential candidate.

    d. called upon all Americans to fight against the English in 1812.

12. During the Napoleonic Wars:
    a. the United States became France's ally.
    b. American neutral rights were violated by Britain.
    c. the United States used impressment to seize French sailors on the high seas.
    d. France and England boycotted all American commerce.

13. The leader of the pan-Indian resistance movement that was defeated at Tippecanoe was:
    a. Tecumseh.
    b. Pontiac.
    c. Metacom.
    d. Sitting Bull

14. The Missouri Compromise:
    a. revealed deep sectional differences in the United States, especially over issues dealing with slavery.
    b. established a plan that would gradually emancipate all the slaves over a period of three generations.
    c. provided a realistic resolution to sectional differences and helped usher in the Era of Good Feelings.
    d. allowed slavery in Missouri but prohibited any states admitted after 1820 from becoming slave states.

15. The Panic of 1819:
    a. was caused by a British invasion of New England.
    b. almost led to a civil war between the Federalists and Republicans.
    c. was exacerbated by "wildcat" state banks that made loans far beyond their resources.
    d. created great opportunities for small farmers to buy land on credit.

Thought Questions: Think carefully about the following questions or comments. Your answers should prepare you to participate in class discussions or help you to write an effective essay. In both class discussions and essays you should always support the arguments you make by referring to specific examples and historical evidence. You may use the space provided to sketch out ideas or outline your response.

1. What European powers continued to hold claims in the Americas in the years following the Revolution? Where were those territories, and how did they influence American history?

2. What were the ideals that shaped the Jeffersonian presidency, and how did his policies advance or retard the implementation of those ideals?

3. Discuss the origins of the War of 1812. What were the principle disagreements between the United States and Britain during the years preceding the war? What role did US relations with Indian peoples play in the coming of this war?

4. What was the American system that men like Henry Clay and John Quincy Adams advocated? Why did this program for economic development come about in the wake of the War of 1812?

5. What were the major issues that made the Missouri Compromise necessary? How was this impasse solved, and what implications did this debate have for the future of the nation?

Map Skills: These questions are based on the maps in the chapter. Please use the blank map provided here for your answers.

1. On the map below identify the boundaries for the major powers of North America in 1800: The United States, Britain, Spain, Russia.

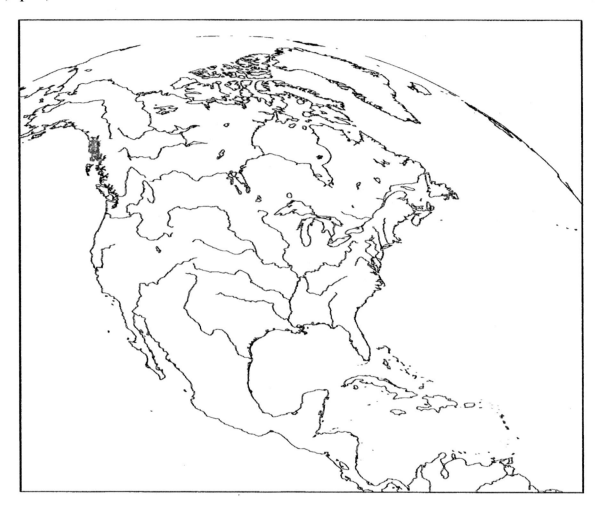

2. Identify these locations that were significant in the American campaigns against Indians: Fallen Timbers, Fort Dearborn, The Thames, Tippecanoe, Fort Mims, and Horseshoe Bend. Identify as well the territory Indian tribes lost as a result of the various campaigns.

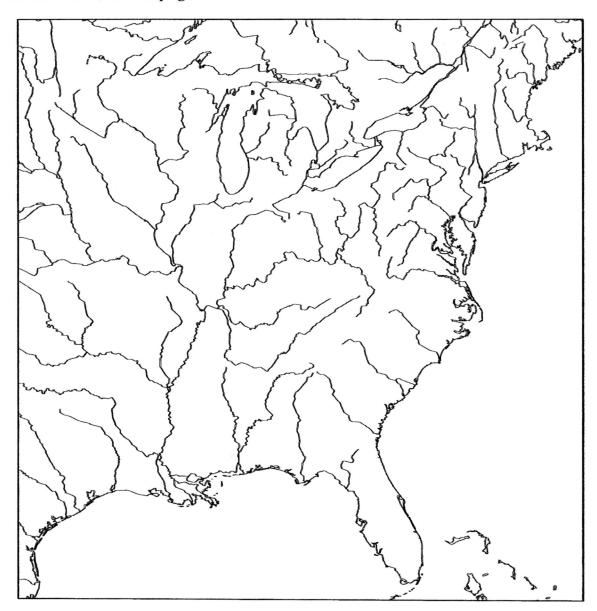

Interpreting the Past

Name _____ Date _____

Analyze the circumstances leading up to the Missouri Compromise.

DOCUMENT 1

An African American Calls for an End to Slavery (1791)
Source: The History Net: African American History,
http://afroamhistory.about.com/library/blbanneker_letter.htm

Maryland, Baltimore County, August 19, 1791.
SIR,
...Sir, if these are sentiments of which you are fully persuaded, I hope you cannot but acknowledge, that it is the indispensable duty of those, who maintain for themselves the rights of human nature, and who possess the obligations of Christianity, to extend their power and influence to the relief of every part of the human race, from whatever burden or oppression they may unjustly labor under; and this, I apprehend, a full conviction of the truth and obligation of these principles should lead all to. Sir, I have long been convinced, that if your love for yourselves, and for those inestimable laws, which preserved to you the rights of human nature, was founded on sincerity, you could not but be solicitous, that every individual, of whatever rank or distinction, might with you equally enjoy the blessings thereof; neither could you rest satisfied short of the most active effusion of your exertions, in order to their promotion from any state of degradation, to which the unjustifiable cruelty and barbarism of men may have reduced them...
And now, Sir, I shall conclude, and subscribe myself, with the most profound respect, Your most obedient humble servant,
BENJAMIN BANNEKER.

DOCUMENT 2

An African American Calls for an End to Slavery (1791)
Source: The History Net: African American History
http://afroamhistory.about.com/library/blbanneker_letter.htm

To Mr. BENJAMIN BANNEKER.
Philadelphia, August 30, 1791.
SIR,
I THANK you, sincerely, for your letter of the 19th instant, and for the Almanac it contained. No body wishes more than I do, to see such proofs as you exhibit, that nature has given to our black brethren talents equal to those of the other colors of men; and that the appearance of the want of them, is owing merely to the degraded condition of their existence, both in Africa and America. I can add with truth, that no body wishes more ardently to see a good system commenced, for raising the condition, both of their body and mind, to what it ought to be, as far as the imbecility of their present existence, and other circumstances, which cannot be neglected, will admit.

I have taken the liberty of sending your Almanac to Monsieur de Condozett, Secretary of the Academy of Sciences at Paris, and Member of the Philanthropic Society, because I considered it as a document, to which your whole color had a right for their justification, against the doubts which have been entertained of them.

I am with great esteem, Sir, Your most obedient Humble Servant,

THOMAS JEFFERSON.

DOCUMENT 3

Thomas Jefferson Reacts to the "Missouri Question" (1820)
Source: Library of Congress, Thomas Jefferson Papers, Series 1. General Correspondence.
1651–1827,
Thomas Jefferson to John Holmes, April 22, 1820,
http://memory.loc.gov

Monticello, April 22, 1820

...The cession of that kind of property, for so it is misnamed, is a bagatelle which would not cost me a second thought, if, in that way, a general emancipation and expatriationcould be effected; and gradually, and with due sacrifices, I think it might be. But as it is, we have the wolf by the ears, and we can neither hold him, nor safely let him go. Justice is in one scale, and self-preservation in the other. Of one thing I am certain, that as the passage of slaves from one state to another would not make a slave of a single human being who would not be so without it, so their diffusion over a greater surface would make them individually happier, and proportionally facilitate the accomplishment of their emancipation, by dividing the burden on a greater number of coadjutors. An abstinence too, from this act of power, would remove the jealousy excited by the undertaking of Congress to regulate the condition of the different descriptions of men composing a state. This certainly is the exclusive right of every state, which nothing in the Constitution has taken from them and given to the general government. Could Congress, for example, say that the non-freemen of Connecticut shall be freemen, or that they shall not emigrate into any other state?

DOCUMENT 4

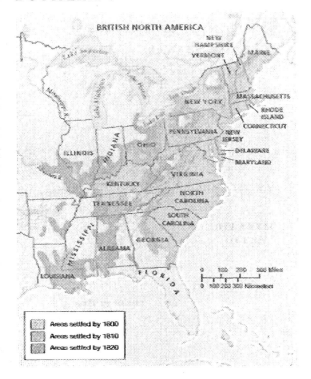

BRITISH NORTH AMERICA

Areas settled by 1800
Areas settled by 1810
Areas settled by 1820

DOCUMENT 5

Source: "Memoirs of a Monticello Slave, as Dictated to Charles Campbell by Isaac" (1847)

… Mr. Jefferson had a clock in his kitchen at Monticello; never went into the kitchen except to wind up the clock. He never would have less than eight covers at dinner if nobody at table but himself. Had from eight to thirty-two covers for dinner. Plenty of wine, best old Antigua rum and cider; very fond of wine and water. Isaac never heard of his being disguised in drink. He kept three fiddles; played in the afternoons and sometimes arter supper. This was in his early time. When he begin to git so old, he didn't play. Kept a spinnet made mostly in shape of a harpsichord; his daughter played on it. Mr. Fauble, a Frenchman that lived at Mr. Walker's, a music man, used to come to Monticello and tune it. There was a fortepiano and a guitar there. Never seed anybody play on them but the French people. Isaac never could git acquainted with them; could hardly larn their names. Mr. Jefferson always singing when ridin' or walkin'; hardly see him anywhar outdoors but what he was a-singin'. Had a fine clear voice, sung minnits (minuets) and sich; fiddled in the parlor. Old Master very kind to servants.

DOCUMENT 6

DOCUMENT 7

Source: Constitutionality of the Louisiana Purchase (1803)
Thomas Jefferson to John C. Breckinridge

Monticello, Aug. 12, 1803
DEAR SIR,-
...Our information as to the country is very incompleat; we have taken measures to obtain it in full as to the settled part, which I hope to receive in time for Congress. The boundaries, which I deem not admitting question, are the high lands on the western side of the Mississippi enclosing all it's waters, the Missouri of course, and terminating in the line drawn from the northwestern point of the Lake of the Woods to the nearest source of the Missipi, as lately settled between Gr Britain and the U S. We have some claims to extend on the sea coast Westwardly to the Rio Norte or Bravo, and better, to go Eastwardly to the Rio Perdido, between Mobile & Pensacola, the antient boundary of Louisiana. These claims will be a subject of negociation with Spain, and if, as soon as she is at war, we push them strongly with one hand, holding out price in the other, we shall certainly obtain the Floridas, and all in good time. In the meanwhile, without waiting for permission, we shall enter into the exercise of the natural right we have always insisted on with Spain, to wit, that of a nation holding the upper part of streams, having a right of innocent passage thro' them to the ocean. We shall prepare her to see us practise on this, & she will not oppose it by force.

DOCUMENT 8

Source: "The Western Country," Extracts from Letters Published in Niles' Weekly Register (1816)

The western country continues to rise in population and importance with unabated rapidity. This town has been, since the war, full to overflowing; many being obliged to leave it after coming from the Eastern states, not being able to get a room to dwell in. More houses will be built this summer than during the last three years together. Manufactories of several important kinds are establishing, among which is a steam grist and saw mill. The surveyor general is making arrangements for laying out, agreeably to late acts of Congress, towns at the Lower Rapids of Sandusky, and at the Rapids of the Miami of the Lakes. The local situation of the latter cannot but render it a most important place. It will be situated at some point within the reservation of twelve miles square, to which vessels of a small tonnage can ascend, and as near the foot of the rapids as may be. I believe the time not very distant when the wealth and resources of the western country will be brought almost to your doors, by means of an extensive inland navigation through the lakes and the grand canal proposed to be made in New York. It will be an easy matter to connect the Miami of the Lakes and the Miami of the Ohio by a canal, the face of the country between the head of the navigation of each of those rivers being quite level. What an extensive inland navigation would then be opened!-from New Orleans to the Hudson!

10. THE SOUTH AND SLAVERY, 1790-1850s

CHAPTER OVERVIEW

Summary

Between 1790 and 1850 the United States expanded westward at a steady pace, bringing many new states into the union. As the United States grew in the South, so did the institution of slavery. Slavery expanded into the new territories of the old southwest because of the increasing significance of cotton cultivation for the region. Eli Whitney's patented device allowed for cotton to become enormously profitable and fueled economic growth throughout the nation. However, while the cotton economy benefited many Americans North and South, it also created important differences that led to growing tensions between the two regions. The expansion of slavery fueled by cotton also wreaked havoc on African American slaves, as many were forced from their homes and families to undertake the tremendous labor needed to turn frontier lands into functioning plantations and farms. The enslaved weathered this storm by clinging to family and community relations, Black Christianity, and outright resistance when the pressures proved too great. In turn, white Southerners of all classes clung ever tighter to the protection that slavery provided them and articulated a defense of slavery that increasingly became a centerpiece of Southern life and politics.

Focus Questions

1. How did attitudes in the South toward slavery change after the invention of the cotton gin?

2. What is a "slave society"?

3. What was life like for slaves in the American South?

4. What role did religion play in African American slave communities?

5. What were the values of yeoman farmers?

6. Who were the planter elite?

7. Why was the white South increasingly defensive after 1830?

CHAPTER REVIEW

Short Response: Consider these questions thoughtfully. Respond with the best possible short answer by filling in the blank.

1. _____ defended slavery by arguing that all societies have an underclass who will always be subordinate to some segment of the population and that slavery, unlike wage labor, protected the enslaved from want in old age and when employment is lacking.

2. _____ argued that slaveholders hoodwinked non-slaveholding Southerners into accepting poverty and ignorance and called for those in the South who owned no slaves to embrace abolition.

3. Eli Whitney's gin was responsible for the explosion in _____ cultivation throughout much of the lower South.

4. By the time of the Civil War, cotton accounted for almost _____ percent of American exports, representing a total value of nearly _____ a year.

5. The _____ developed as aspiring planters sought to purchase increasing numbers of slaves to work on the new lands developed in the southwest of the early nineteenth century.

6. The transatlantic slave trade to the United States was ended by Congress in _____.

7. _____ of all slaves were designated as field hands.

8. _____, which swept the South after the 1760s, introduced many slaves to Christianity, often in mixed congregations with white people.

9. In 1831, _____ actually started a slave rebellion in which a number of white people were killed, which greatly increased Southern fears.

10. The word _____ originally a British term for a farmer who works his own land, is often applied to independent farmers of the South, most of whom lived on family-sized farms.

Multiple Choice: Select the response that best answers the question or best completes the sentence.

1. Alabama Fever is best described as:
   a. a lower South malady that wiped out large numbers of white and black Southerners in the 1830s.
   b. a sickness that affected only African Americans because of a weakened immune system.
   c. the frenzied pursuit of land and cotton cultivation that struck many Americans in the early nineteenth century.
   d. the reaction of many people to the discovery of gold deposits along the Tennessee River.

2. The significance of the cotton gin was:
   a. that it improved the way that cotton was planted.
   b. its ability to kill pests that could plague a crop.
   c. that it sped up the process by which cotton was cleaned.
   d. that it allowed cotton to be grown easily in upper South states like Virginia.

3. As a result of large-scale cotton production in the South:
   a. capital in the region was concentrated in land and slaves.
   b. most Southerners came to own large numbers of slaves.
   c. a sophisticated infrastructure emerged to help market the crop.
   d. the region was so wealthy that there were no poor white southerners.

4. Which Southern politician famously declared cotton to be King in 1858?:
   a. Whitey Ford of Indiana.
   b. James Gillispie of Virginia
   c. Henry Clay of Kentucky.
   d. James Henry Hammond of South Carolina.

5. The connection between Southern slavery and Northern industry:
   a. did not survive the American Revolution.
   b. was very direct and included significant ties between slaveholders and textile, shipping, and brokerage interests.
   c. was severed because of tensions over slavery.
   d. could never fully develop because of the incompatibility between slavery and free labor.

6. As a result of the internal slave trade:
   a. nearly one million slaves were forced to relocate to new lands in the South.
   b. most Southern legislatures passed laws to prohibit the separation of families.
   c. many slaves from the lower South were sold into upper South slave markets.
   d. the transatlantic slave trade was reopened in 1838.

7. One result of the slaves' existence was:
   a. that they never really developed a sense of family or kinship.
   b. small families that resulted from malnutrition and poor health.
   c. the emergence of families based solely on African traditions.
   d. the development of strong familial and non-kinship relationships.

8. Between 1790 and 1860 the slave population:
   a. declined steadily because of maltreatment.
   b. grew from approximately 700,000 to 4,000,000.
   c. was concentrated in the Southern states west of the Mississippi River like Louisiana.
   d. grew only because of the steady importation of Africans.

9. In the South during the years prior to 1850:
   a. free African Americans experienced tremendous social and racial discrimination.
   b. all the African Americans were held as either slaves or indentured servants.
   c. free African Americans enjoyed social equality but did not have the right to vote.
   d. the only economic opportunities available to free African Americans were as farmers.

10. From 1790 until the 1840s:
   a. most Southerners owned either a large or small plantation, and the planter class was the largest to own slaves.
   b. the largest group of slave owners were small independent farmers hoping to improve their economic circumstances.
   c. although few Southerners owned large numbers of slaves, almost all white males owned at least one bondsman.
   d. most slaves lived on small farms that operated with just a few slaves, who usually worked alongside their owners.

11. All of the following is true of house servants in the Old South except:
   a. they remained under the scrutiny of masters even more so than field hands .
   b. they were generally better fed and clothed.
   c. they were among the few slaves who did not run away during the Civil War.
   d. had greater access to information about the world from listening to white conversations.

12. All of the following were nineteenth century slave revolts or plots except:
   a. the Stono Rebellion.
   b. Gabriel Prosser's insurrection.
   c. the Denmark Vesey plot.
   d. Nat Turner's Rebellion.

13. Most Southern yeoman farmers:
   a. owned large numbers of slaves.
   b. valued personal independence over economic gain.
   c. hated slavery because they derived no benefit from it.
   d. sought to maximize their income by taking significant risks in market competition.

14. Beginning in the 1830s:
   a. the defense of slavery became the overwhelming current in southern society.
   b. more and more southerners came to see slavery as morally reprehensible.
   c. an open debate over slavery became the defining characteristic of southern politics.
   d. an increasing number of southerners sought ways to resolve their differences with the North.

15. In regard to slavery, the Constitution of the United States:
   a. was silent and offered the institution no protection.
   b. was a strongly anti-slavery document.
   c. provided slave owners their greatest legal defense.
   d. was neutral by design in order to maintain regional peace.

Thought Questions: Think carefully about the following questions or comments. Your answers should prepare you to participate in class discussions or help you to write an effective essay. In both class discussions and essays you should always support the arguments you make by referring to specific examples and historical evidence. You may use the space provided to sketch out ideas or outline your response.

1. Describe slavery in the United States late in the 1790s, and discuss how the institution developed once the cotton boom began.

2. Define several elements that helped shape the growth of an African-American community among the slaves. How was that community similar to white culture? How did the slave community differ from white society?

3. Why did differing groups of white Southerners accept or support slavery? What were some of the principle arguments used by these groups to defend the institution?

Map Skills: These questions are based on the maps in the chapter. Please use the blank map provided here for your answers.

1. Identify the regions of the South where cotton cultivation was of the greatest importance. Identify which areas of the South also had the greatest and least concentrations of slaves within their populations.

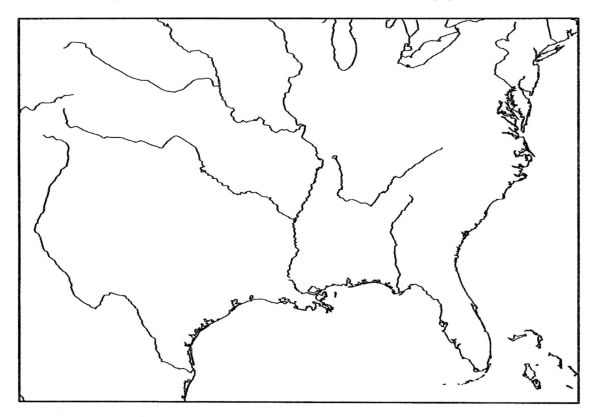

2. Demonstrate the progression of western expansion in the US South from the American Revolution until 1850 by identifying which states were among the original thirteen, were admitted by 1821, or entered the union by 1850. In addition, identify the major routes of the internal slave trade that helped populate these newer areas.

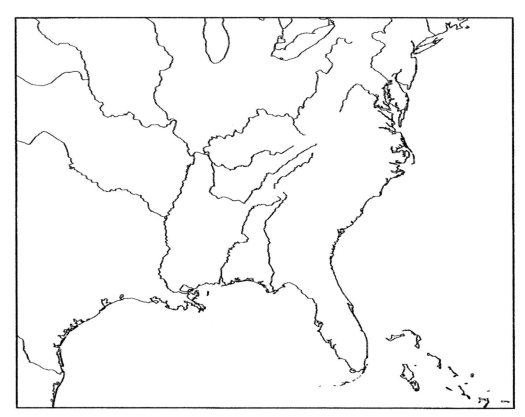

Interpreting the Past

Name _____ **Date** _____

Discuss the role of paternalism in the southern slave system.

DOCUMENT 1

Source: State v. Boon (1801)

JOHNSTON, J. The murder of a slave, appears to me, a crime of the most atrocious and barbarous nature; much more so than killing a person who is free, and on an equal footing. It is an evidence of a most depraved and cruel disposition, to murder one, so much in your power, that he is incapable of making resistance, even in his own defence ...and had there been nothing in our acts of Assembly, I should not hesitate on this occasion to have pronounced sentence of death on the prisoner.

DOCUMENT 2

A Black Abolitionist Speaks Out (1829)
Source: PBS Online, Africans in America.
http://cgi.pbs.org/wgbh/aia/part4/4h2931t.html

My dearly beloved Brethren and Fellow Citizens:
. . . to my no ordinary astonishment, [a] Reverend gentleman got up and told us (coloured people) that slaves must be obedient to their masters—must do their duty to their masters or be whipped—the whip was made for the backs of fools, &c. Here I pause for a moment, to give the world time to consider what was my surprise, to hear such preaching from a minister of my Master, whose very gospel is that of peace and not of blood and whips, as this pretended preacher tried to make us believe. What the American preachers can think of us, I aver this day before my God, I have never been able to define.

DOCUMENT 3

Nat Turner, Confession (1831)
Source: From Thomas R. Gray, The Confessions of Nat Turner, The Leader of the Late Insurrection in Southamton Virginia (Baltimore, 1831).

Several years rolled round, in which many events occurred to strengthen me in this my belief. At this time I reverted in my mind to the remarks made of me in my childhood, and the things that had been shewn me-and as it had been said of me in my childhood by those by whom I had been taught to pray, both white and black, and in whom I had the greatest confidence, that I had too much sense to be raised, and if I was, I would never be of any use to any one as a slave. Now finding I had arrived to man's estate, and was a slave, and these revelations being made known to me, I began to direct my attention to this great object, to fulfill the purpose for which, by this time, I felt assured I was intended.

DOCUMENT 4

An Abolitionist Defends the Amistad Mutineers (1839)

Source: Exploring Amistadat Mystic Seaport,
http://amistad.mysticseaport.org/library/news/journal.of.commerce.html

Sabbath evening. The Rev. H. G. Ludlow prayed for the poor Africans this forenoon, very feelingly, at the service in his church. The outer door of the jail was closed today, and visitors generally were not admitted. I distributed some religious tracts, in the morning, to the convicts, and attempted to instruct the African prisoners, especially the children. They pronounce words in English very distinctly, and have already nearly the numerals. In showing them some books containing pictures of tropical animals, birds, &c., they seemed much pleased to recognize those with whose appearance they were acquainted, endeavoring to imitate their voices and actions. With suitable instruction these intelligent and docile Africans would soon learn to read and speak our language, and I cannot but hope that some of the benevolent inhabitants of this city will diligently continue to improve the opportunity to impart instruction to these pagans, brought by the providence of God to their very doors.

DOCUMENT 5

Source: De Bow's Review, "The Stability of the Union," (1850)

In this undisturbed progress, the condition of the black race is being elevated on the swelling tide of white progress. Inasmuch as that the first slaves imported were, under their new masters, vastly superior in condition to the nude cannibals by whom they were sold, only because avarice triumphed over appetite so is the condition of the slave of the present day far above that of his progenitor a few generations back. The black race, in its servitude to the whites, has undergone an improvement, which the same race, in its state of African freedom, has failed to manifest. By whatever degree, physically and morally, the blacks of the United States are superior to the nude cannibals of Africa, are they indebted to the white race for its active, though not disinterested agency. That process of improvement has not ceased, but is ever progressive in the train of white advancement.

DOCUMENT 6

Source: Benjamin Drew, Narratives of Escaped Slaves (1855)

[Mrs. James Steward]
I am from the eastern shore of Maryland. I never belonged but to one master; he was very bad indeed. I was never sent to school, nor allowed to go to church. They were afraid we would have more sense than they. I have a father there, three sisters, and a brother. My father is quite an old man, and he is used very badly. Many a time he has been kept at work whole long summer day without sufficient food. A sister of mine has been punished by his taking away her clothes and locking them up, because she used to run when master whipped her. He kept her at work with only what she could pick up to tie on her for decency. He took away her child which had just begun to walk, and gave it to another woman-but she went and got it afterward. He had a large farm eight miles from home. Four servants were kept at the house. My master could not manage to whip my sister when she was strong. He waited until she was confined, and the second week after her confinement he said, "Now I can handle you, now you are weak." She ran from him, however, and had to go through water, and was sick in consequence.

DOCUMENT 7

DOCUMENT 8

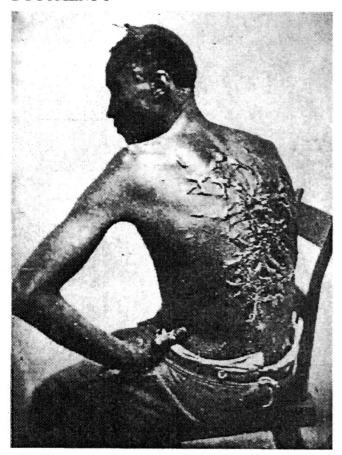

11. THE GROWTH OF DEMOCRACY, 1824-1840

CHAPTER OVERVIEW

Summary

The period between 1824 and 1840 is often considered the "Age of the Common Man." This assertion rests on the fact that during this period most white adult males gained the right to vote without having to meet traditional property or taxpaying requirements. While far from being a truly democratic society, the young United States did enjoy greater public participation in the electoral process and witnessed the birth of a Second Party System, marked by growing national parties. Andrew Jackson represented many of the attributes celebrated or opposed by political parties of this era. In fact, Jackson's views on issues like the Bank of the United States and nullification would color American politics for many years to come. In addition, the celebration of the common American experience gave rise to artistic attempts to carve out a distinctive national identity. These artistic efforts often focused on romanticized visions of the natural environment and the American's place within the New World. However, while Americans attempted to define a national identity through expanding politics, migration, and artistic achievement, others like free blacks and the Five Civilized Tribes saw themselves pushed figuratively and literally further outside of American society through whites only voting policies and forced Indian removal.

Focus Questions

1. How did suffrage expand between 1800 and 1840?

2. In what ways did Andrew Jackson's presidency affirm the new democratic politics?

3. How did the major political struggles of the Jackson years strengthen the executive branch of government?

4. How did the basic two-party pattern of American political democracy take shape?

5. How was a distinctive American cultural identity shaped by writers and artists?

CHAPTER REVIEW

Short Response: Consider these questions thoughtfully. Respond with the best possible short answer by filling in the blank.

1. The _____ of Philadelphia was one way that many skilled workers responded to the economic changes that the Market Revolution brought about in the United States.

2. The inauguration of President _____ attracted "[t]housands and thousands of people, without distinction of rank" and was a reflection of growing democratization within the US.

3. By 1840, more than _____ percent of the adult white male population of the United States could vote.

4. Prior to 1800 most of the original thirteen states denied the vote to all except _____.

5. Disappointed supporters of Andrew Jackson described the outcome of the 1824 election as a _____.

6. In New York State, master political tactician _____ forged a tightly organized, broad-based political group nicknamed the Albany Regency that wrested political control away from the former elite.

7. Andrew Jackson's election in 1828 ushered in a new era in American politics, an era that historians have called the _____.

8. Andrew Jackson's cabinet was divided over his overt support for _____, the beautiful, flamboyant wife of his Secretary of War.

9. Because of his ability to forge political compromises, _____ of Kentucky was known as the "Great Pacificator."

10. John C. Calhoun defended the doctrine of _____ in his "Exposition and Protest" written in 1828.

Multiple Choice: Select the response that best answers each question or best completes each sentence.

1. The Second American Party System:
    a. was a political confrontation between Federalists and Republicans.
    b. strengthened the political environment that had developed during the 1790s.
    c. created truly national political parties for the first time in American history.
    d. grew out of differences of opinion over America's role in international affairs.

2. Following its independence from Spain, Mexico:
    a. sought to become a part of the United States but was refused admission to the union.
    b. achieved remarkable stability and became an insurmountable obstacle to US expansion.
    c. struggled to rebuild its economy and maintain balance between competing factions.
    d. was invited to join the United States as four separate states.

3. Which of the following was not helpful in extending the right to vote during the Jacksonian Era:
    a. the War of 1812.
    b. the admission of new western states.
    c. a decline in prejudice against women and non-white persons.
    d. all of the above.

4. In the election of 1824 Andrew Jackson won the largest share of popular and electoral votes but ultimately lost the presidency to:
   a. Henry Clay.
   b. John C. Calhoun.
   c. Martin Van Buren.
   d. John Quincy Adams.

5. A manifestation of popular democratic culture of the nineteenth century was:
   a. an increasingly active popular press.
   b. participation in parades.
   c. the wearing of party regalia and singing of songs or slogans.
   d. all of the above.

6. Andrew Jackson's popularity rested on all of the following characteristics except:
   a. being born into a powerfully connected family.
   b. his military record.
   c. his tough reputation.
   d. his rise from humble origins to become a wealthy man.

7. In comparison to previous presidents, Andrew Jackson:
   a. was hesitant to assert presidential authority on national issues.
   b. used the presidential veto quite frequently.
   c. actively sought the advice of his cabinet.
   d. sought to remove the influence of the masses from policymaking.

8. The Nullification Crisis:
   a. was the first time in American history that one section of the nation expressed strong disagreement with national policies.
   b. grew out of economic differences between eastern and western states and had little to do with the Constitution.
   c. revealed that the southern states were more committed to preserving the Union than were the New England States.
   d. epitomized growing sectional differences and the constitutional questions associated with those differences.

9. The state at the center of the Nullification Crisis was:
   a. Mississippi.
   b. South Carolina.
   c. North Carolina.
   d. Georgia.

10. The Cherokee received a favorable ruling against the policy of Indian Removal in which court case:
    a. McCulloch v. Maryland.
    b. Marybury v. Madison.
    c. Jackson v. Ross.
    d. Worchester v. Georgia.

11. The proposals that Henry Clay advocated came to be known as:
    a. the New Nationalism.
    b. the American System.
    c. the Age of Democracy.
    d. the Industrial Revolution.

12. President Andrew Jackson:
    a. replaced the Bank of the United States with the national Federal Reserve System.
    b. tried to resist the efforts by Henry Clay to destroy the Bank of the United States.
    c. generally mistrusted banks and so moved to destroy the Bank of the United States.
    d. had no interest in banks and refused to take a position on the Bank of the United States.

13. The political coalition that emerged in opposition to the Jacksonian Democrats was the:
    a. Bucktail Party.
    b. Federalist Party.
    c. Republican Party.
    d. Whig Party.

14. The Panic of 1837:
    a. refers to a suspected slave revolt in Alabama.
    b. partly resulted from the expiration of the Bank of the United States.
    c. benefited Martin Van Buren's reelection bid.
    d. was relatively mild and short lived.

15. Expansion, freedom of the common man, limitation of government authority were all major positions of which mid-nineteenth century political party?:
    a. Democrats.
    b. Republican.
    c. Federalist.
    d. Whig.

Thought Questions: Think carefully about the following questions or comments. Your answers should prepare you to participate in class discussions or help you to write an effective essay. In both class discussions and essays you should always support the arguments you make by referring to specific examples and historical evidence. You may use the space provided to sketch out ideas or outline your response.

1. Discuss how the presidential elections of the 1820s reflected the growing importance of popular democracy in American politics. How did those elections influence the advent of the Age of Democracy? Was this truly the "Age of the Common Man"? Explain why that was or was not the case.

2. What were the most important issues of Andrew Jackson's presidency? Explain his stance on the issues. How and why, if at all, did Jackson's policy positions contribute to the celebration of the common man?

3. What were the major differences between the competitors in the Second American Party System? Explain who were the principal supporters for these two parties and describe the general reasons behind their party affiliation.

4. What were the central ideas behind the policy of Indian Removal? How was this policy carried out in the face of tribal and Supreme Court Opposition? What does this policy suggest about the nature of presidential authority during the Age of Jackson?

Map Skills: These questions are based on the maps in the chapter. Please use the blank map provided here for your answers.

1. Locate the areas of the United States that had the highest concentration of population in 1830. Which areas of the South and the West had the highest population density? What factors do you think influenced population patterns as the United States expanded to the West?

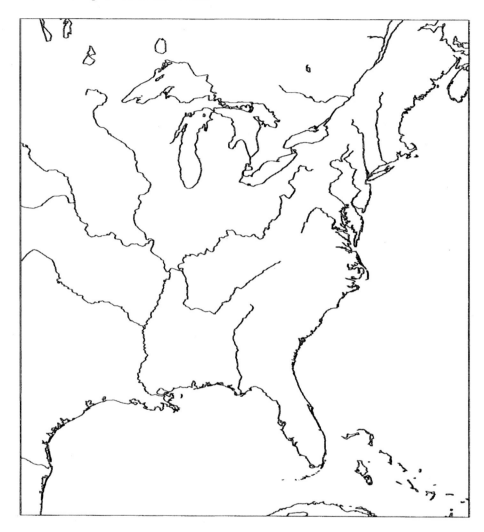

2. Compare the election results from 1824 and 1828. Identify which areas of the country voted for each candidate in those elections. Do you see any evidence of the growth of national party appeal in the outcome of either election?

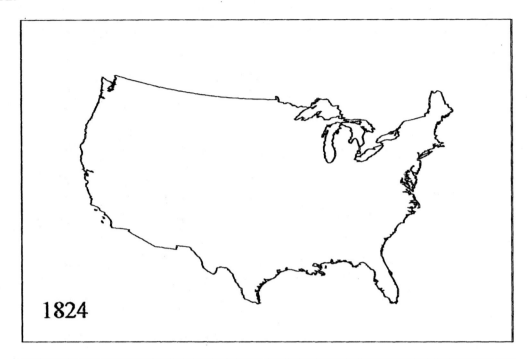

1824

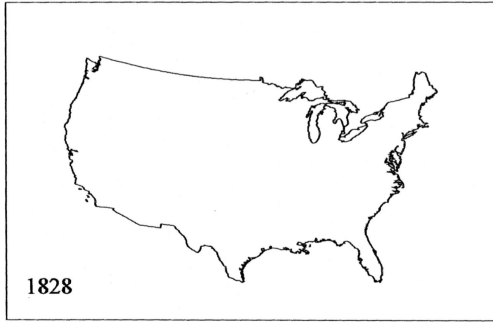

1828

3. Locate the areas of the South that Indian tribes ceded to the United States in the 1830s. Where were the tribes that ceded the lands ultimately located?

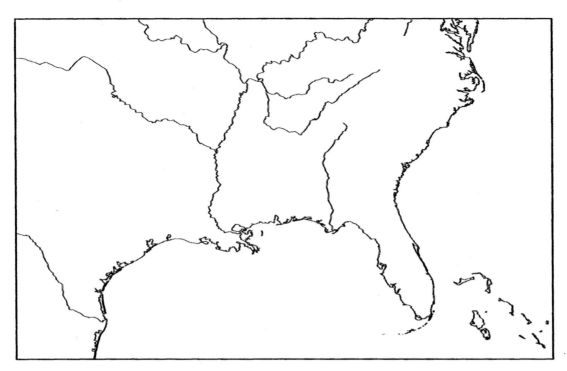

Interpreting the Past

Name _____ Date _____

   The Jacksonian Era is often described as a time when the United States experienced the "democratization of politics." Is this accurate? How was democracy defined in this era?

DOCUMENT 1

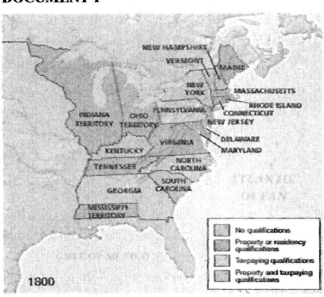

DOCUMENT 2

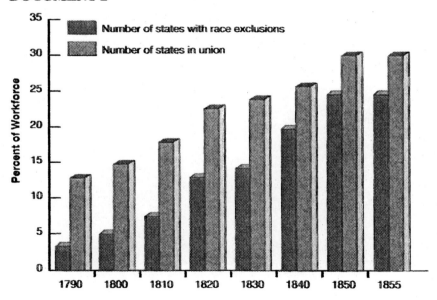

DOCUMENT 3

A "Corrupt Bargain" or Politics as Usual? (1824)
Source: Charles Francis Adams, ed. Memoirs of John Quincy Adams, 12 Volumes (Philadelphia: J. B. Lippincott & Co., 1875).

9th. . . . Mr. Clay came at six, and spent the evening with me in a long conversation explanatory of the past and prospective of the future. He said that the time was drawing near when the choice must be made in the House of Representatives of a President from the three candidates presented by the electoral colleges; that he had been much urged and solicited with regard to the part in that transaction that he should take, and had not been five minutes landed at his lodgings before he had been applied to by a friend of Mr. Crawford's, in a manner so gross that it had disgusted him; that some of my friends also, disclaiming, indeed, to have any authority from me, had repeatedly applied to him, directly or indirectly, urging considerations personal to himself as motives to his cause. He had thought it best to reserve for sometime his determination to himself: first, to give a decent time for his own funeral solemnities as a candidate; and, secondly, to prepare and predispose all his friends to a state of neutrality between the three candidates who would be before the House, so that they might be free ultimately to take that course which might be most conducive to the public interest. The time had now come at which he might be explicit in his communication with me, and he had for that purpose asked this confidential interview. He wished me, as far as I might think proper, to satisfy him with regard to some principles of great public importance, but without any personal considerations for himself. In the question to come before the House between General Jackson, Mr. Crawford, and myself, he had no hesitation in saying that his preference would be for me.

18th. (…) Mr. S. L. Southard came, to ask for the papers he had left with me yesterday, of which Mr. Kirkpatrick wishes to take copies. I gave them to him. He then asked me some questions respecting the election, upon which I spoke to him with entire confidence. I asked him if he wished me so to speak to him, and he said he did. I told him of the present state of things, so far as it is known to myself; of the present prospect, that a majority of the friends of Mr. Clay and Mr. Crawford would finally vote for me, but that the whole of the aspect may be changed from day to day.

Feb. 4. . . . I delivered to the President the letter I had written him yesterday upon the subject of the nominations to the foreign missions, and told him that I wished to put it as a deposit in his hands, for a testimonial that I had not used those missions to promote any purpose of my own.

Feb. 12. . . . General Brown entered this morning into an argument to convince me that it would not be expedient that Mr. Clay should be Secretary of State. He had a high opinion of Mr. Clay, but if I should offer him the Department he hoped he would not accept it, and he believed it would be better if I should not offer it to him. General Brown wished that De Witt Clinton should be the Secretary of State. I listened to what he said, and then told him I had already made the offer to Mr. Clay…

DOCUMENT 4

Andrew Jackson, First Annual Message to Congress (1829)
Source: From Messages and Papers of the Presidents, ed. J. D. Richardson, National Archives and Records Administration, (1896), II, 456-459 (Dec. 8, 1829).

The condition and ulterior destiny of the Indian tribes within the limits of some of our states have become objects of much interest and importance. It has long been the policy of government to introduce among them the arts of civilization, in the hope of gradually reclaiming them from a wandering life. This policy has, however, been coupled with another wholly incompatible with its success. Professing a desire to civilize and settle them, we have at the same time lost no opportunity to purchase their lands and thrust them farther into the wilderness. By this means they have not only been kept in a wandering state, but been led to look upon us as unjust and indifferent to their fate....

Our conduct toward these people is deeply interesting to our national character. Their present condition, contrasted with what they once were, makes a most powerful appeal to our sympathies. Our ancestors found them the uncontrolled possessors of these vast regions. By persuasion and force they have been made to retire from river to river and from mountain to mountain, until some of the tribes have become extinct and others have left but remnants to preserve for awhile their once terrible names...I suggest for our consideration the propriety of setting apart an ample district west of the Mississippi, and without [outside] the limits of any state or territory now formed, to be guaranteed to the Indian tribes as long as they shall occupy it, each tribe having a distinct control over the portion designated for its use. There they may be secured in the enjoyment of governments of their own choice, subject to no other control from the United States than such as may be necessary to preserve peace on the frontier and between the several tribes...This emigration should be voluntary, for it would be as cruel as unjust to compel the aborigines to abandon the graves of their fathers and seek a home in a distant land. But they should be distinctly informed that if they remain within the limits of the states they must be subject to their laws.

DOCUMENT 5

Source: "Memorial of the Cherokee Nation" (1830)

We are aware that some persons suppose it will be for our advantage to remove beyond the Mississippi. We think otherwise. Our people universally think otherwise. Thinking that it would be fatal to their interests, they have almost to a man sent their memorial to Congress, deprecating the necessity of a removal. . . . It is incredible that Georgia should ever have enacted the oppressive laws to which reference is here made, unless she had supposed that something extremely terrific in its character was necessary in order to make the Cherokees willing to remove. We are not willing to remove; and if we could be brought to this extremity, it would be not by argument, nor because our judgment was satisfied, not because our condition will be improved; but only because we cannot endure to be deprived of our national and individual rights and subjected to a process of intolerable oppression.
We wish to remain on the land of our fathers. We have a perfect and original right to remain without interruption or molestation. The treaties with us, and laws of the United States made in pursuance of treaties, guaranty our residence and our privileges, and secure us against intruders. Our only request is, that these treaties may be fulfilled, and these laws executed.

DOCUMENT 6

Source: Andrew Jackson, Veto of the Bank Bill (1832)

To the Senate:

The bill "to modify and continue" the act entitled "An act to incorporate the subscribers to the Bank of the United States" was presented to me on the 4th July instant. Having considered it with that solemn regard to the principles of the Constitution which the day was calculated to inspire, and come to the conclusion that it ought not to become a law, I herewith return it to the Senate, in which it originated, with my objections...

I sincerely regret that in the act before me I can perceive none of those modifications of the bank charter which are necessary, in my opinion, to make it compatible with justice, with sound policy, or with the Constitution of our country.

The present corporate body, denominated the president, directors, and company of the Bank of the United States, will have existed at the time this act is intended to take effect twenty years. It enjoys an exclusive privilege of banking under the authority of the General Government, a monopoly of its favor and support, and, as a necessary consequence, almost a monopoly of the foreign and domestic exchange. The powers, privileges, and favors bestowed upon it in the original character, by increasing the value of the stock far above its par value, operated as a gratuity of many millions to the stockholders. . . .

It is not conceivable how the present stockholders can have any claim to the special favor of the Government. The present corporation has enjoyed its monopoly during the period stipulated in the original contract. If we must have such a corporation, why should not the Government sell out the whole stock and thus secure to the people the full market value of the privileges granted? Why should not Congress create and sell twenty-eight millions of stock, incorporating the purchasers with all the powers and privileges secured in this act and putting the premium upon the sales into the Treasury?

But this act does not permit competition in the purchase of this monopoly. It seems to be predicated on the erroneous idea that the present stockholders have a prescriptive right not only to the favor but to the bounty of Government. It appears that more than a fourth part of the stock is held by foreigners and the residue is held by a few hundred of our own citizens, chiefly of the richest class. For their benefit does this act exclude the whole American people from competition in the purchase of this monopoly and dispose of it for many millions less than it is worth. This seems the less excusable because some of our citizens not now stockholders petitioned that the door of competition might be opened, and offered to take a charter on terms much more favorable to the Government and country. . . .

It is to be regretted that the rich and powerful too often bend the acts of government to their selfish purposes. Distinctions in society will always exist under every just government. Equality of talents, of education, or of wealth can not be produced by human institutions. In the full enjoyment of the gifts of Heaven and the fruits of superior industry, economy, and virtue, every man is equally entitled to protection by law; but when the laws undertake to add to these natural and just advantages artificial distinctions, to grant titles, gratuities, and exclusive privileges, to make the rich richer and the potent more powerful, the humble members of society-the farmers, mechanics, and laborers-who have neither the time nor the means of securing like favors to themselves, have a right to complain of the injustice of their Government.

DOCUMENT 7

Source: The Force Bill (1833)

SEC. 5. And be it further enacted, That whenever the President of the United States shall be officially informed, by the authorities of any state, or by a judge of any circuit or district court of the United States, in the state, that, within the limits of such state, any law or laws of the United States, or the execution thereof, or of any process from the courts of the United States, is obstructed by the employment of military force, or by any other unlawful means, too great to be overcome by the ordinary course of judicial proceeding, or by the powers vested in the marshal by existing laws, it shall be lawful for him, the President of the United States, forthwith to issue his proclamation, declaring such fact or information, and requiring all such military and other force forthwith to disperse; and if at any time after issuing such proclamation, any such opposition or obstruction shall be made, in the manner or by the means aforesaid, the President shall be, and hereby is, authorized, promptly to employ such means to suppress the same, and to cause the said laws or process to be duly executed . . .

DOCUMENT 8

A French Traveler Reports on American Society (1835)
Source: Alexis de Tocqueville, Democracy in America, Volume 2 (American Studies at the University of Virginia, Hypertexts) http://xroads.virginia.edu/~HYPER/DETOC/ch2_05.htm

The political associations that exist in the United States are only a single feature in the midst of the immense assemblage of associations in that country. Americans of all ages, all conditions, and all dispositions constantly form associations. They have not only commercial and manufacturing companies, in which all take part, but associations of a thousand other kinds, religious, moral, serious, futile, general or restricted, enormous or diminutive. The Americans make associations to give entertainments, to found seminaries, to build inns, to construct churches, to diffuse books, to send missionaries to the antipodes; in this manner they found hospitals, prisons, and schools. If it is proposed to inculcate some truth or to foster some feeling by the encouragement of a great example, they form a society. Wherever at the head of some new undertaking you see the government in France, or a man of rank in England, in the United States you will be sure to find an association...Thus the most democratic country on the face of the earth is that in which men have, in our time, carried to the highest perfection the art of pursuing in common the object of their common desires and have applied this new science to the greatest number of purposes. Is this the result of accident, or is there in reality any necessary connection between the principle of association and that of equality?
(...)
Nothing, in my opinion, is more deserving of our attention than the intellectual and moral associations of America. The political and industrial associations of that country strike us forcibly; but the others elude our observation, or if we discover them, we understand them imperfectly because we have hardly ever seen anything of the kind. It must be acknowledged, however, that they are as necessary to the American people as the former, and perhaps more so. In democratic countries the science of association is the mother of science; the progress of all the rest depends upon the progress it has made.
Among the laws that rule human societies there is one which seems to be more precise and clear than all others. If men are to remain civilized or to become so, the art of associating together must grow and improve in the same ratio in which the equality of conditions is increased.

12. INDUSTRY AND THE NORTH, 1790s–1840s

CHAPTER OVERVIEW

Summary

During the first half of the nineteenth century, the United States underwent a revolution with regard to the transportation and manufacture of goods. These changes were gradual and were most pronounced in the North, centered along major water and railway routes. Innovations like McCormick's reaper and the American System of Manufactures greatly increased the productive capacity of farmers and workers and forever changed longstanding approaches to agriculture and artisanry. The expansion of commercial farming and wage labor in the North opened new avenues for individuals to earn great wealth, but simultaneously increased a person's vulnerability to difficult economic times and poor decision making. While many did not eagerly embrace these changes, the efficiency and profitability of the new modes of production encouraged entrepreneurs to press ever forward. The emerging individualism of the marketplace was reinforced by the development of free labor ideology and the revitalization of evangelical Christianity, which became central pillars of the new middle class family. In time, the shift away from older, household-based modes of production led to the development of a society that was becoming increasingly different from that of the rural, slave society of the South. These differences would soon become major impediments to maintaining peace between the two regions.

Focus Questions

1. What were the effects of the Transportation Revolution?

2. What was the market revolution?

3. How did industrialization affect workers in early factories?

4. How did the market revolution change the lives of ordinary people?

5. What were the values of the new middle class?

CHAPTER REVIEW

Short Response: Consider these questions thoughtfully. Respond with the best possible short answer by filling in the blank.

1. One of the first cotton textile mills in the United States which hired young, unmarried women to manufacture cloth was located in _____, _____.

2. The _____ was the first major federal internal improvement project which contributed to the Transportation Revolution.

3. The _____ was the highly successful effort to link the Great Lakes with New York City.

4. The steamboat was first developed by _____ in 1807.

5. The first railroad in the United States was the _____ and opened in 1830 with 13 miles of track.

6. The _____ caused major changes throughout the United States and resulted from rapid improvements in transportation, commercialization, and industrialization.

7. On of the first steps towards industrialization was the _____, which entailed having people manufacture goods at home under the indirect supervision of a merchant.

8. The first steel plow was invented by _____ in 1837 and cut plowing time in half.

9. _____ was a British apprentice whose keen memory allowed him to the copy the advanced technology of English textile mills and thereby improve the industrial capabilities of the United States.

10. The _____ was an important industrial innovation in that it allowed for easy assembly and repair of items through the development of standardized parts.

Multiple Choice: Select the response that best answers each question or best completes each sentence.

1. A major difference between pre-industrial production and factory work was:
   a. that only adult family members worked in the factories.
   b. the precise and unrelenting work schedule in factories.
   c. that prior to industrialism, workers never received wages.
   d. the way workers were given a voice in setting work conditions.

2. Many women workers were attracted to working at Lowell Mills:
   a. in an effort of escape rural isolation and gain exposure to city life.
   b. because they were paid as much as male employees.
   c. since it was a way to earn money prior to getting married.
   d. a & c.
   e. all of the above.

3. The revolutionary transportation development of the 1820s was:
   a. the Erie Canal.
   b. the Yankee Clipper.
   c. a transcontinental railroad.
   d. the creation of the national highway.

4. One major result of the transportation revolution was:

a. a sharp reduction in the average number of hours worked by Americans.

b. an infrastructure that tied all regions of the nation directly to New York City.

c. a surprising rise in the cost of moving goods from the east to the west.

d. it linked Americans to larger communities of interest.

5. All of the following were cities that sprung up along the Erie Canal except:

a. Utica.

b. Rochester.

c. Buffalo.

d. Albany.

6. The emergence of the market economy:

a. eliminated poverty in most regions of the United States.

b. helped encourage expansion into the western territories.

c. had little influence outside of the manufacturing Northeast.

d. spread to all areas of the country within just a few years.

7. The Yankee West:

a. refers to Midwestern regions settled by relocating New Englanders.

b. was a famous schooner that shipped Southern cotton to international markets.

c. was a cattle herding region of upstate New York which provided beef to urban markets.

d. refers to the "wild" behavior of entrepreneurs in Northern financial markets.

8. The commercialization of agriculture in the Old Northwest:

a. was resisted by a vast majority of the regional population.

b. led to crop specialization as farmers sought to maximize yields and profits.

c. reinforced older patterns of household production.

d. was hindered by the transportation revolution.

9. The expansion of corn and hog farming in the Midwest led to which city becoming know as "Porkopolis"?:

a. New Orleans.

b. Memphis.

c. Chicago.

d. Cincinnati.

10. During the years 1790 through 1840:

a. religion generally strengthened and reinforced the emerging middle-class values characteristic of the market revolution.

b. the social dislocations associated with the Industrial Revolution led to a decline in church attendance in the United States.

c. most religious leaders criticized industrialism because the impersonality of the factory system undermined Christian compassion.

d. the first religious revival in American history occurred as workers looked for ways to ease the transition to the market economy.

11. As a result of the Market Revolution, Artisans:

a. were able to command higher wages for the increasing number of skilled craftsmen who dominated manufacturing.

b. enjoyed greater economic security.

c. in most crafts lost control of production and were reduced to wage laborers.

d. eagerly embraced the productivity of industrialization.

12. Workers in the new factories of the nineteenth century United States had to adjust of all the following except:
    a. the pace of the work.
    b. the repetition of the work.
    c. an increasing emphasis on clock time.
    d. the blending of home and work.

13. The Second Great Awakening:
    a. undercut the impact of industrialization by downplaying the role of individuals in matters of faith.
    b. supported the labor movement's call for protecting workers against exploitation.
    c. reinforced free labor ideology by emphasizing the power of individual conversion experiences.
    d. led to widespread legislation barring women and children from working in factories.

14. The new middle class family of the nineteenth century:
    a. divided household responsibilities between home and work spheres.
    b. was predominantly found in the South where family values were strongest.
    c. was profoundly criticized by Catherine Beecher in her Treatise on Domestic Economy.
    d. had more children because the new economy provided them with greater resources.

15. Ralph Waldo Emerson's *Walden* is most reflective of which intellectual movement:
    a. sentimentalism.
    b. anarchism.
    c. transcendentalism.
    d. Marxism.

Thought Questions: Think carefully about the following questions or comments. Your answers should prepare you to participate in class discussions or help you to write an effective essay. In both class discussions and essays you should always support the arguments you make by referring to specific examples and historical evidence. You may use the space provided to sketch out ideas or outline your response.

1. Describe pre-industrial methods of production. How did those methods reflect and influence social and familial relations in the United States? How did those relationships change with the coming of factories?

2. Discuss the four major means of transportation that developed early in the 1800s. How did each of them help bring about a revolution in the movement of goods and people?

3. Discuss the processes of commercialization and industrialization as well as the American System of Manufacturing. How did these developments impact the opportunities for artisans and wage laborers in the nineteenth century?

4. Discuss the increasing importance of individualism in American life that resulted from the Market Revolution. What impact did the concept of free labor, the Second Great Awakening, and middle class family life have on the perceived roles and responsibilities of individuals in society?

Map Skills: These questions are based on the maps in the chapter. Please use the blank map provided here for your answers.

1. Locate the major transportation links that emerged in the early 1800s. What does the transportation system reveal about the growth of northern industry? Can you draw any conclusions concerning how the transportation system might have influenced sectional differences between the North and the South?

Interpreting the Past

Name _____ Date _____

Defend or refute the following statement: The market revolution was an unmitigated good for the American People.

DOCUMENT 1

The Case for the Erie Canal
Source: David Hosack, Memoir of De Witt Clinton(New York: J. Seymour, 1829),
http://www.history.rochester.edu/canal/bib/hosack/APPOT.html

> ...When completed, this would afford a course of navigation from New-York, by sloop navigation to Albany, 160 miles—from Albany to Buffalo, by boat navigation, 300 miles—from Buffalo to Chicago by sloop navigation, 1200 miles; making a distance of 1600 miles of inland navigation up stream, where the cargo has to be shifted but three times.

The probable charges of freight would be—from New-York to Albany (the present price on small packages of merchandise up freight is about) five dollars per ton, from thence to Buffalo (full large enough, including no charge for lockage) fifty dollars a ton, from thence to Chicago, say large fifty dollars per ton—is equal to 105 dollars per ton, or five cents per pound nearly. From Chicago harbour it might be continued up its river, by portage, into and down the Illinois, and up the Mississippi; and into, as yet, almost unknown regions.

The navigation of the four largest lakes in the known world, together with all their tributary streams—the agricultural products and the commerce of all the surrounding country, would pass through this canal—and even the fifth (Ontario) would become its tributary.—The additional duty on the Canadian trade alone would defray the annual repairs of the canal.

The vast extension of and facility to commerce, together with the additional spur to industry which this canal would give, would in twenty years redeem the principal and interest of their expenditure, at the rate of their present imposts, by its additional increase.

Its invitation to the culture of the fertile soil surrounding these extensive navigable waters, would be such, that in a few generations the exhibition of their improvements and the display of their wealth, would even scarcely be equaled by the old world.

DOCUMENT 2

Source: Henry Clay, "Defense of the American System" (1832)

I have now to perform the more pleasing task of exhibiting an imperfect sketch of the existing state of the unparalleled prosperity of the country. On a general survey, we behold cultivation extended, the arts flourishing, the face of the country improved; our people fully and profitably employed; and the public countenance exhibiting tranquility, contentment and happiness. And if we descend into particulars, we have the agreeable contemplation of a people out of debt, land rising slowly in value, but in a secure and salutary degree; a ready though not extravagant market for all the surplus productions of our industry; innumerable flocks and herds browsing and gamboling on ten thousand hills and plains, covered with rich and verdant grasses; our cities expanded, and whole villages springing up, as it were, by enchantment; our exports and imports increased and increasing; our tonnage, foreign and coastwise, swelling and fully occupied; the rivers of our interior animated by the perpetual thunder and lightning of countless steam-boats; the currency sound and abundant; the public debt of two wars nearly redeemed; and, to crown all, the public treasury overflowing, embarrassing Congress, not to find subjects of taxation, but to select the objects which shall be liberated from the impost. If the term of seven years were to be selected, of the greatest prosperity which this people have enjoyed since the establishment of their present constitution, it would be exactly that period of seven years which immediately followed the passage of the tariff of 1824.

DOCUMENT 3

Source: The Harbinger, Female Workers of Lowell (1836)

In Lowell live between seven and eight thousand young women, who are generally daughters of farmers of the different states of New England. Some of them are members of families that were rich in the generation before. . .

The operatives work thirteen hours a day in the summer time, and from daylight to dark in the winter. At half past four in the morning the factory bell rings, and at five the girls must be in the mills. A clerk, placed as a watch, observes those who are a few minutes behind the time, and effectual means are taken to stimulate to punctuality. This is the morning commencement of the industrial discipline (should we not rather say industrial tyranny?) which is established in these associations of this moral and Christian community.

At seven the girls are allowed thirty minutes for breakfast, and at noon thirty minutes more for dinner, except during the first quarter of the year, when the time is extended to forty-five minutes. But within this time they must hurry to their boardinghouses and return to the factory, and that through the hot sun or the rain or the cold. A meal eaten under such circumstances must be quite unfavorable to digestion and health, as any medical man will inform us. After seven o'clock in the evening the factory bell sounds the close of the day's work.

Thus thirteen hours per day of close attention and monotonous labor are extracted from the young women in these manufactories. . . . So fatigued-we should say, exhausted and worn out, but we wish to speak of the system in the simplest language-are numbers of girls that they go to bed soon after their evening meal, and endeavor by a comparatively long sleep to resuscitate their weakened frames for the toil of the coming day.

DOCUMENT 4

Source: James F. Cooper, Notions of the Americans (1840)

The construction of canals, on a practical scale, the mining for coal, the exportation of cotton goods, and numberless other improvements, which argue an advancing state of society, have all sprung into existence within the last dozen years. It is a knowledge of these facts, with a clear and sagacious understanding of their immense results, coupled with the exciting moral causes, that render the American sanguine, aspiring, and confident in his anticipations. He sees that his nation lives centuries in an age, and he feels no disposition to consider himself a child, because other people, in their dotage, choose to remember the hour of his birth.

DOCUMENT 5

DOCUMENT 6

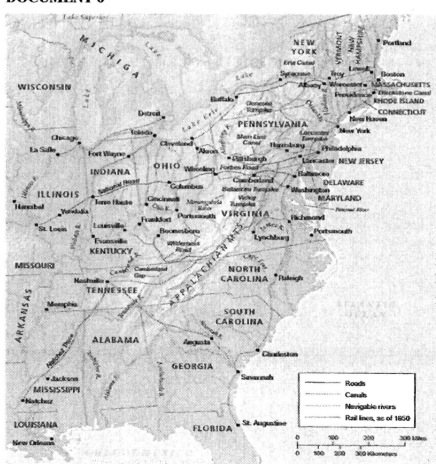

Roads
Canals
Navigable rivers
Rail lines, as of 1850

DOCUMENT 7

DOCUMENT 8

TIME TABLE OF THE LOWELL MILLS,

To take effect on and after Oct. 21st, 1851.

The Standard time being that of the meridian of Lowell, as shown by the regulator clock of JOSEPH RAYNES, 43 Central Street.

January,	5.00	6.00	6.50	*7.30	5.00	6.00	6.50	*7.30	5.00	6.00	6.50	*7.30
February,	4.30	5.30	6.40	*7.30	4.30	5.30	6.25	*7.30	4.30	5.30	6.15	*7.30
March,	5.40	6.00		*7.30	5.30	5.40		*7.30	5.20			6.35
April,	4.45	5.00		6.45	4.30	5.00		6.55	4.30	4.30		7.00
May,	4.30	4.30		7.00	4.30	4.30		7.00	4.30	4.30		7.00
June,												
July,												
August,												
September,	4.40	5.00		6.45	4.40	5.00		6.30	5.00	5.00		*7.30
October,	5.10	5.30		*7.30	5.30	5.40		*7.30	5.35	5.30		*7.30
November,	4.30	5.30	6.10	*7.30	4.30	5.30	6.20	*7.30	4.30	5.00	6.00	6.15	*7.30
December,	5.00	6.00	6.45	*7.30	5.00	6.00		*7.30	5.00	6.00	6.00	6.50	*7.30

* Excepting on Saturdays from Sept. 21st to March 20th inclusive, when it is rung at 20 minutes after sunset.

YARD GATES,

Will be opened at ringing of last morning bell, of meal bells, and of evening bells; and kept open Ten minutes.

MILL GATES.

Commence hoisting Mill Gates, Two minutes before commencing work.

WORK COMMENCES,

At Ten minutes after last morning bell, and at Ten minutes after bell which "rings in" from Meals.

BREAKFAST BELLS.

During March "Ring out"............at.....7.30 a. m..........."Ring in" at 8.05 a. m.
April 1st to Sept. 20th inclusive.....at.....7.00 " " .... " " at 7.35 " "
Sept. 21st to Oct. 31st inclusive.....at.....7.30 " " .... " " at 8.05 " "
Remainder of year work commences after Breakfast.

DINNER BELLS.

"Ring out"..........................12.30 p. m..........."Ring in"..... 1.05 p. m.

In all cases, the first stroke of the bell is considered as marking the time.

DOCUMENT 9

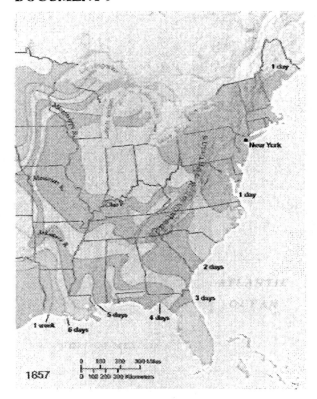

DOCUMENT 10

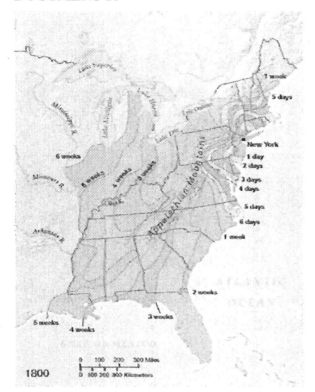

1800

13. MEETING THE CHALLENGES OF THE NEW AGE, 1820s–1850s

CHAPTER OVERVIEW

Summary

The Market Revolution steadily and dramatically changed the urban landscape of the nineteenth century United States. The expansion of industry and commerce attracted ever increasing numbers of people into the nation's cities and many new cities sprung up out of seemingly nothing. Among this influx of people were substantial numbers of new immigrants whose cultures and habits were often frowned upon or deemed threatening. Cultural and ethnic tensions were further exacerbated by the daunting challenges that problems like crime, poor sanitation, overcrowding, and periodic recession could have on these growing population centers. Many urban residents, particularly the native-born and middle class, turned to reform movements in order to minimize the problems of urban life and improve the nation's prospects for continued success. Out of these efforts new, enthusiastic and controversial movements like abolition and the call for women's rights would be born. The uncompromising nature of some of these organizations fueled tensions in places already hotly competitive along social, economic, religious, and cultural lines. At times these tensions could, and did, erupt in violence, thereby disrupting the peace that many sought to create. Nonetheless, despite such persistent challenges, idealists and activists held strongly to their views and continued pressing for positive change.

Focus Questions

1. What caused the immigration of the 1840s and 1850s, and what were responses to it?

2. Why were cities so unable to cope with rapid urbanization?

3. What motivated reform movements?

4. What were the origins and political effects of the abolitionist movement?

5. How were women involved in reform efforts?

CHAPTER REVIEW

Short Response: Consider these questions thoughtfully. Respond with the best possible short answer by filling in the blank.

1. The _____ was the petition considered by the participants who attended the women's rights convention at Seneca Falls in 1848.

2. The Seneca Falls participant who proposed that the convention consider supporting voting rights for women was _____.

3. Prior to the convening of the women's rights convention, member of the Seneca Falls were also quite active in other reform movements like _____.

4. By 1860, _____ had the largest urban population in the United States.

5. The city of _____ handled about 50% of the nation's cotton exports by 1860.

6. By 1860 the population of New York City was _____ percent foreign-born.

7. One of the biggest factors behind the wave of Irish immigration to the United States was the _____ of 1849-1849.

8. The _____ attracted many new immigrants to the west coast of the United States including thousands of Chinese workers and prospectors.

9. Poor sanitation and crowded living conditions in the rapidly growing cities of the United States led to repeated instances of deadly and costly _____.

10. Evangelical minister Charles G. Finney preached the doctrine of _____ through which he believed the whole world could be reformed and redeemed.

Multiple Choice: Select the response that best answers each question or best completes each sentence.

1. The *Declaration of Sentiments* produced by the Seneca Falls Convention in 1848:
   a. was heartily supported by most major newspapers of the day.
   b. was modeled after the Declaration of Independence.
   c. decried women activists for breaking with traditional gender norms.
   d. was actually written by a man.

2. The emerging market revolution:
   a. was most noticeable in the rural areas of America.
   b. had its most noticeable impact in American cities.
   c. changed the American economy but not the society.
   d. was the result of powerful social reform movements.

3. As large numbers of immigrants arrived in the United States after 1820:
   a. the new arrivals quickly and fully assimilated into traditional American culture and society.
   b. they broke with traditional culture and embraced completely new ways of living.
   c. they continued to practice their native religion, but gave up other customs and traditions.
   d. they often settled in neighborhoods of people who shared their native culture and concepts.

4. One result of the rapid growth of American cities during this period was:
   a. the deepening of sharp class differences.
   b. the virtual elimination of poverty in the nation.
   c. a cosmopolitan attitude toward newcomers.

d. an effort to ensure equal economic opportunity.

5. Which of the following accurately identifies the four largest cities in the United States in 1860:
   a. New York City, Philadelphia, Boston, Baltimore.
   b. New York City, New Orleans, Boston, Baltimore.
   c. Philadelphia, Boston, Charleston, New York City.
   d. Philadelphia, New York City, Baltimore, Charleston.

6. The American labor movement:
   a. began as workers grew disenchanted with political parties' failure to address important issues.
   b. was a broad-based effort that included men and women from all sectors of the economy.
   c. experienced rapid early growth as unskilled workers joined unions to protect their interests.
   d. weakened dramatically as the emerging market economy provided good, high-paying jobs.

7. All of the following provided important streams of immigration to the United States from 1820 to 1850 except:
   a. West Africans.
   b. the Irish.
   c. Germans.
   d. the Chinese.

8. All of the following were characteristics of growing US cities in the nineteenth century except:
   a. poor sanitation.
   b. ethnic and class segregation.
   c. a declining gap between rich and poor.
   d. middle class movement toward the suburbs.

9. The temperance movement:
   a. resulted in a sharp drop in the per capita consumption of alcohol.
   b. led to the prohibition of alcohol in most states by the early 1850s.
   c. had little effect on the social behavior and drinking habits of Americans.
   d. remained within the middle class and did not attract working-class support.

10. The Burned Over District of upstate New York:
    a. refers to an area of the state that was prone to major fires before the development of professional fire fighting companies.
    b. refers to a region plagued by pro and anti-immigrant riots.
    c. was a region that was heavily influenced by the reform movements of the nineteenth century.
    d. was so heavily farmed that its soil was rapidly depleted or "burned."

11. Between 1820 and 1860 all of the following cities were rocked by Anti-black violence except:
    a. Philadelphia, PA.
    b. Birmingham, AL.
    c. Cincinnati, OH.
    d. New York City.

12. Which of the following was an important force behind the reform movements of the nineteenth century?:
    a. the spread of evangelical Christianity.
    b. the growth in the Middle Class.
    c. concerns about the problems of rapidly growing cities.
    d. all of the above.
    e. a & c only.

13. Sabbatarianism:
    a. was a new religion led by Joseph Smith.
    b. was universally accepted as being supportive of traditional family values.
    c. led to protests among some working people when businesses and taverns were closed on Sundays.
    d. was opposed by most evangelical Christians as being too "Catholic."

14. Which of the following was an outspoken leader of the abolitionists?
    a. James Henry Hammond.
    b. William Lloyd Garrison.
    c. Henry Clay.
    d. John Humphrey Noyes.

15. All of the following were major undertakings by the abolitionist movement except:
    a. the publication of the Liberator.
    b. unanimous support for the American Colonization Society.
    c. the founding of the Liberty Party.
    d. participation in the Underground Railroad.

Thought Questions: Think carefully about the following questions or comments. Your answers should prepare you to participate in class discussions or help you to write an effective essay. In both class discussions and essays you should always support the arguments you make by referring to specific examples and historical evidence. You may use the space provided to sketch out ideas or outline your response.

1. Describe the major patterns of immigration between 1820 and 1850. What impact did this period of immigration have on the urban landscape? Why were many native-born Americans alarmed by the arrival of some immigrant groups?

2. Describe the major features of urban life in the mid-nineteenth century United States. Identify and describe some of the major difficulties that urban residents had to face during this era.

3. Identify and describe some of the major reform movements that emerged within the United States during the 1820s and 1850s. What were some of the major influences that shaped the goals and activities of these movements?

4. Discuss the emergence of the abolitionist movement. Why did it develop at this time? How was it received by the general population and what were some major impediments abolitionists faced in attempting to end slavery?

5. Discuss the connections between the emergence of nineteenth century reform movements and the origin of a women's rights movement. Who supported this movement and what might have led them to take this stand?

Map Skills: These questions are based on the maps in the chapter. Please use the blank map provided here for your answers.

1. Identify the areas of the United States where major immigrant groups had settled by 1860. Why did immigrants target these areas for settlement?

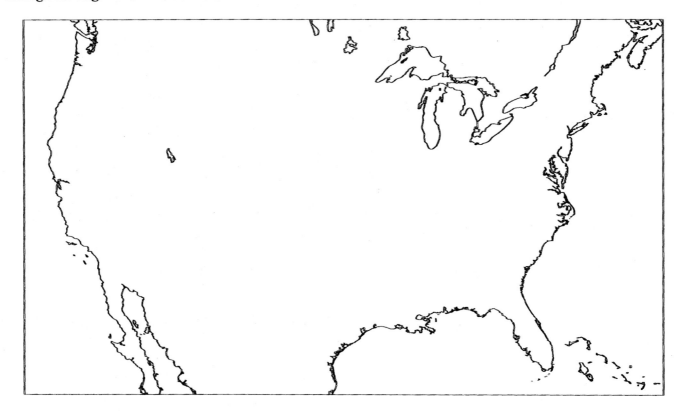

2. Locate the Burned-Over District and the various reform movements that occurred there. Can you detect any connection between the growth of reform movements and the Market Revolution in this pattern that emerges?

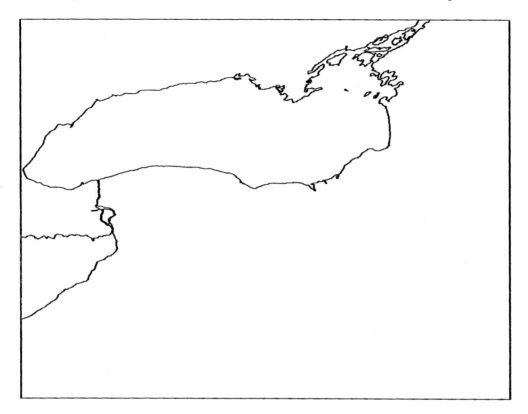

Interpreting the Past

Name _____ **Date** _____

What concerns and challenges did reformers confront in the antebellum era, and how did they address them?

DOCUMENT 1

DOCUMENT 2

THE DRUNKARDS PROGRESS.

FROM THE FIRST GLASS TO THE GRAVE.

DOCUMENT 3

Source: Charles Finney, "What a Revival of Religion Is" (1835)

It is altogether improbable that religion will ever make progress among heathen nations except through the influence of revivals. The attempt is now making to do it by education, and other cautious and gradual improvements. But so long as the laws of mind remain what they are, it cannot be done in this way. There must be excitement sufficient to wake up the dormant moral powers, and roll back the tide of degradation and sin. And precisely so far as our own land approximately to heathenism, it is impossible for God or man to promote religion is such a state of things but by powerful excitements.- This is evident from the fact that this has always been the way in which God has done it. God does not create these excitements, and choose this method to promote religion for nothing, or without reason. Where mankind are so reluctant to obey God, they will not obey until they are excited. For instance, how many there are who know that they ought to be religious, but they are afraid if they become pious they will be laughed at by their companions. Many are wedded to idols, others are procrastinating repentance, until they are settled in life, or until they have secured some favorite worldly interest. Such persons never will give up their false shame, or relinquish their ambitious schemes, till they are so excited that they cannot contain themselves any longer. . . . It is presupposed that the church is sunk down in a backslidden state, and a revival consists in the return of the church from her backsliding, and in the conversion of sinners.

DOCUMENT 4

A Lowell Mill Girl Tells her Story (1836)
Source: Internet Modern History Sourcebook, http://www.fordham.edu/halsall/mod/
robinson-lowell.html

The early mill girls were of different ages. Some were not over ten years old; a few were in middle life, but the majority were between the ages of sixteen and twenty-five. The very young girls were called "doffers." They "doffed," or took off, the full bobbins from the spinning frames, and replaced them with empty ones. These mites worked about fifteen minutes every hour and the rest of the time was their own. When the overseer was kind they were allowed to read, knit, or go outside the mill yard to play. They were paid two dollars a week. The working hours of all the girls extended from five o'clock in the morning until seven in the evening, with one half hour each, for breakfast and dinner. Even the doffers were forced to be on duty nearly fourteen hours a day. This was the greatest hardship in the lives of these children. Several years later a ten hour law was passed, but not until long after some of these little doffers were old enough to appear before the legislative committee on the subject, and plead, by their presence, for a reduction of the hours of labor.

DOCUMENT 5

Souce: "Petition of the Catholics of New York" (1840)

Your petitioners have to state further, as grounds of their conscientious objections to those schools, that many of the selections in their elementary reading lessons contain matter prejudicial to the Catholic name and character. The term "POPERY" is repeatedly found in them. This term is known and employed as one of insult and contempt towards the Catholic religion, and it passes into the minds of children with the feeling of which it is the outward expression. Both the historical and religious portions of the reading lessons are selected from Protestant writers, whose prejudices against the Catholic religion render them unworthy of confidence in the mind of your petitioners, at least so far as their own children are concerned. . . .

For these reasons, and others of the same kind, your petitioners cannot, in conscience, and consistently with their sense of duty to God, and to their offspring, intrust the Public School Society with the office of giving "a right direction to the minds of their children." And yet this Society claims that office, and claims for the discharge of it the Common School Funds, to which your petitioners, in common with other citizens, are contributors. In so far as they are contributors, they are not only deprived to the damage and detriment of their religion, in the minds of their own children, and of the rising generation of the community at large. The contest is between the *guarantied* rights, civil and religious, of the citizen on the one hand, and the pretensions of the Public School Society on the other; and whilst it has been silently going on for years, your petitioners would call the attention of your Honorable Body to its consequences on that class for whom the benefits of public education are most essential-the children of the poor.

DOCUMENT 6

Horace Mann on Education and National Welfare
Source: United States Department of State, International Information Programs,
http://usinfo.state.gov/usa/infousa/facts/democrac/16.htm

Now, surely, nothing but Universal Education can counter-work this tendency to the domination of capital and the servility of labor. If one class possesses all the wealth and the education, while the residue of society is ignorant and poor, it matters not by what name the relation between them may be called; the latter, in fact and in truth, will be the servile dependents and subjects of the former. But if education be equally diffused, it will draw property after it, by the strongest of all attractions; for such a thing never did happen, and never can happen, as that an intelligent and practical body of men should be permanently poor. Property and labor, in different classes, are essentially antagonistic; but property and labor, in the same class, are essentially fraternal. The people of Massachusetts have, in some degree, appreciated the truth, that the unexampled prosperity of the State,—its comfort, its competence, its general intelligence and virtue,—is attributable to the education, more or less perfect, which all its people have received; but are they sensible of a fact equally important?—namely, that it is to this same education that two thirds of the people are indebted for not being, to-day, the vassals of as severe a tyranny, in the form of capital, as the lower classes of Europe are bound to in the form of brute force.

Education, then, beyond all other devices of human origin, is the great equalizer of the conditions of men—the balance-wheel of the social machinery. I do not here mean that it so elevates the moral nature as to make men disdain and abhor the oppression of their fellow-men. This idea pertains to another of its attributes. But I mean that it gives each man the independence and the means, by which he can resist the selfishness of other men. It does better than to disarm the poor of their hostility towards the rich; it prevents being poor. Agrarianism is the revenge of poverty against wealth. The wanton destruction of the property of others,—the burning of hay-ricks and corn-ricks, the demolition of machinery, because it supersedes hand-labor, the sprinkling of vitriol on rich dresses,—is only agrarianism run mad. Education prevents both the revenge and the madness. On the other hand, a fellow-feeling for one's class or caste is the common instinct of hearts not wholly sunk in selfish regards for person, or for family. The spread of education, by enlarging the cultivated class or caste, will open a wider area over which the social feelings will expand; and, if this education should be universal and complete, it would do more than all things else to obliterate factitious distinctions in society.

DOCUMENT 7

Declaration of Sentiments and Resolutions, Woman's Rights Convention,
Seneca Falls, New York (1848)
Source: E. C. Stanton, S. B. Anthony, and Matilda Joslyn Gage, eds., History of Woman Suffrage, vol. 1
(Rochester, NY: Charles Mann, 1881), pp. 70–72.

We hold these truths to be self-evident: that all men and women are created equal; that they are endowed by their Creator with certain inalienable rights; that among these are life, liberty, and the pursuit of happiness; that to secure these rights governments are instituted, deriving their just powers from the consent of the governed. . .. But when a long train of abuses and usurpations, pursuing invariably the same object evinces a design to reduce them under absolute despotism, it is their duty to throw off such government, and to provide new guards for their future security. Such has been the patient sufferance of the women under this government, and such is now the necessity which constrains them to demand the equal station to which they are entitled.

The history of mankind is a history of repeated injuries and usurpations on the part of man toward woman, having in direct object the establishment of an absolute tyranny over her. To prove this, let facts be submitted to a candid world (...)
Now, in view of this entire disfranchisement of one-half the people of this country, their social and religious degradation in view of the unjust laws above mentioned, and because women do feel themselves aggrieved, oppressed, and fraudulently deprived of their most sacred rights, we insist that they have immediate admission to all the rights and privileges which belong to them as citizens of the United States.

DOCUMENT 8

14. THE TERRITORIAL EXPANSION OF THE UNITED STATES, 1830s–1850s

CHAPTER OVERVIEW

Summary

From the 1830s to the 1850s, the concept of manifest destiny became a mantra and eventually a battle cry for a majority of the United States. Americans continued their westward migration throughout this period with trade, scientific curiosity, avarice for mineral wealth, and a surging nationalism, all being major forces driving them to new lands. In the wake of this drive toward westward settlement, the United States pushed aside many longtime inhabitants of these lands. Indians in the east were pushed onto reservations in the Trans-Mississippi West, while Tejanos and Californios became strangers in their ancestral homes once that territory became controlled by the United States. Armed with the firm belief that God had given the lands of North America to their nation, Americans threatened war with Britain over Oregon and waged war against Mexico as ambitious politicians used expansion as a key campaign weapon. However, while winning an election and a war, territory-hungry Democrats unwittingly awakened the dreaded specter of extending slavery into previously free lands. In so doing, the Democrats sowed the seeds for the growth of free soil ideology and began eroding the national party system, which had previously managed to minimize sectional rivalries.

Focus Questions

1. What was manifest destiny?

2. What were the major differences between the Oregon, Texas, and California frontiers?

3. What were the most important consequences of the Mexican-American War?

4. What was the link between expansion and slavery?

5. What were the issues in the election of 1848?

CHAPTER REVIEW

Short Response: Consider these questions thoughtfully. Respond with the best possible short answer by filling in the blank.

1. The Tejano who was with the defenders of the Alamo and later became the mayor of San Antonio in an independent Texas was _____.

2. The Mexican General who was victorious at the Alamo but eventually defeated and forced to grant Texas independence was _____.

3. From 1804 to 1806, _____ led a federal supported expedition to explore and record information about the land and peoples of the western United States.

4. Many Indian tribes from the eastern United States were located across the Mississippi River to a section of the Great Plains that many described as the _____.

5. Members of the Five Civilized Tribes who had been removed from the eastern United States eventually established tribal nations in what today is the state of _____.

6. _____ was a famous American historian who argued that the repeated experience of settling new frontiers across the continent had shaped Americans into a uniquely adventurous, optimistic, and democratic people.

7. The newspaperman who coined the phrase "manifest destiny" was _____.

8. The _____ was the ill-fated wagon train that had to turn to cannibalism after becoming trapped in the mountains while on the Oregon Trail.

9. In 1844, James K. Polk was elected President of the United States after running on a campaign pledge of _____ in regard to the Oregon Territory.

10. The _____ was the path leading to an important New Mexican trading post which attracted much attention from American entrepreneurs and expansion enthusiasts in the nineteenth century.

Multiple Choice: Select the response that best answers each question or best completes each sentence.

1. The Battle of the Alamo:
    a. was over the right to control trade on the Oregon Trail.
    b. was won under the leadership of Davy Crockett.
    c. became a rallying cry for Texans in their pursuit for independence.
    d. forced Mexico to cede California to the United States.

2. Of the ten states admitted to the union from 1800 to 1840:
    a. all but one were west of the Appalachian Mountains.
    b. none were allowed to have slavery.
    c. all were areas seized from Mexico.
    d. only one was west of the Appalachian Mountains.

3. According to expansion supporters of the nineteenth century, the "manifest destiny" of the United States was:
    a. to spread democracy and freedom to all the inhabitants of North America.
    b. to treat all countries as equals in the community of nations.
    c. to show mercy and compassion to people of all races and ethnicity.
    d. that God desired for the nation to dominate all of North America.

4. The joint occupation of Oregon was an agreement between the United States and:
    a. France.

b. Great Britain.

c. Mexico.

d. Russia.

5. Each of the following was an important component of United States westward expansion except:

   a. the fur trade.

   b. federally supported expeditions to explore the region.

   c. desire for expanded trade in Asia.

   d. the treaty with Spain that allowed US trade access to California.

6. All of the following were among the Five Civilized Tribes who were forced to relocate in the West except:

   a. the Choctaw.

   b. the Chickasaw.

   c. the Seminole.

   d. the Comanche.

7. Which political party was in favor of the rapid acquisition and settlement of new territory in the 1840s?:

   a. Federalists.

   b. Liberty Party.

   c. Democrats.

   d. Whigs.

8. The war against Mexico:

   a. had the patriotic support of all the American people.

   b. had the support of Northerners but not Southerners.

   c. generated significant opposition in the United States.

   d. was the first undeclared conflict in American history.

9. The Treaty of Guadalupe Hidalgo:

   a. initially gave the United States most of Mexico, but the U.S. Senate refused to take all the territory.

   b. gave the United States all of the territory west of the boundary established by the Adams-Onís Treaty.

   c. marked the first time that the United States acquired new territory without having to pay anything for it.

   d. set the Texas border at the Rio Grande and ceded California and New Mexico to the United States.

10. President James K. Polk and other expansionists wanted to obtain California:

    a. as an important step to expanding American commerce into Asia.

    b. because of all the gold that the Mexicans had discovered there.

    c. to ensure that Russians would be forced to abandon their colonies.

    d. to make sure that Great Britain's efforts to purchase the territory failed.

11. Once Texas became independent from Mexico:

    a. it was immediately annexed to the United States.

    b. it applied for admission to the United States but was denied entry.

    c. Southern states became concerned over its anti-slavery policies.

    d. John Quincy Adams began a campaign to see it admitted to the Union.

12. The Wilmot Proviso was significant because:

    a. it reopened the debate over slavery and triggered the first rupture of the national party system.

    b. Southern voting blocks were able to ram it through Congress.

    c. it demonstrated that most Americans were unconcerned about the extension of slavery.

    d. it failed to go into force since Congress could not override President Polk's veto.

13. The "free-soil" movement:
    a. was an effort to provide equality for African Americans.
    b. wanted slavery abolished throughout the United States.
    c. proposed giving former slaves land to support themselves.
    d. advocated outlawing the further extension of slavery.

14. President Polk wanted to acquire all of Mexico but was unable to do so:
    a. because of Whig opposition and anti-slavery sentiment.
    b. concerns over adding a large non-white population to the United States.
    c. Mexico's last minute victory over General Scott at Tampico.
    d. a & b
    e. b & c

15. The California Gold Rush was responsible for all the following except:
    a. causing the California population to grow rapidly.
    b. creating diminished population diversity as whites drove all others out of the goldfields.
    c. California being admitted to the Union in 1850.
    d. the development of a corporate-based mining industry in California.

Thought Questions: Think carefully about the following questions or comments. Your answers should prepare you to participate in class discussions or help you to write an effective essay.   In both class discussions and essays you should always support the arguments you make by referring to specific examples and historical evidence. You may use the space provided to sketch out ideas or outline your response.

1. Discuss how economic and political considerations encouraged American westward expansion. How did that expansion affect Indians and other inhabitants of the West?

2. Define manifest destiny and explain how and why it came to be an accepted idea among most Americans. Discuss how the American experience prior to the 1840s had set the stage for Manifest Destiny.

3. How did those Americans who supported a war against Mexico justify the conflict? What was the basis for the opposition of those who were against the war?

4. Describe the concepts behind the Wilmot Proviso and the Free-Soil Movement. Who supported or opposed the ideas represented by these two developments and why might they have done so?

Map Skills: These questions are based on the maps in the chapter. Please use the blank map provided here for your answers.

1. Identify Indian Country, the Oregon Country, Canada, the Republic of Texas, Mexican Territory, and the area disputed by Texas and Mexico in 1840 on the map below.

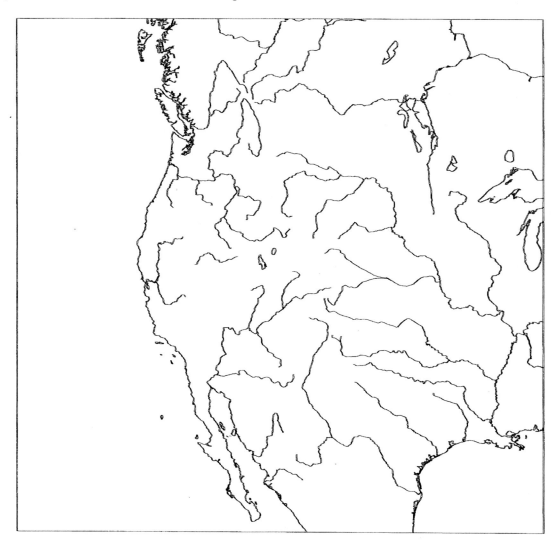

2. Identify the territorial boundaries of Canada, the United States, and Mexico as of 1850. How has the map changed from the one of 1840 above? What precipitated these changes?

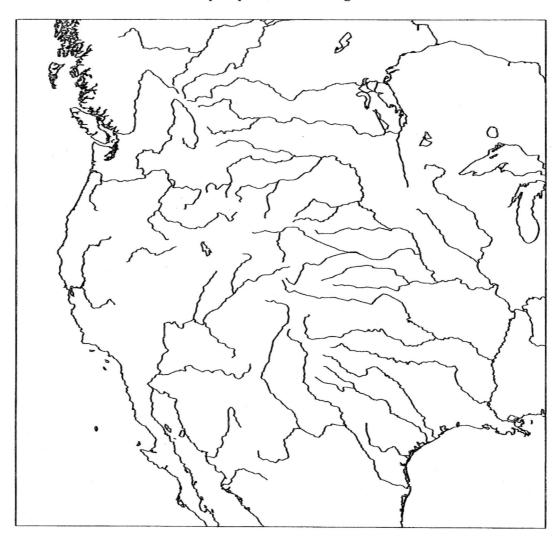

3. Identify the major campaigns that occurred during the war against Mexico.

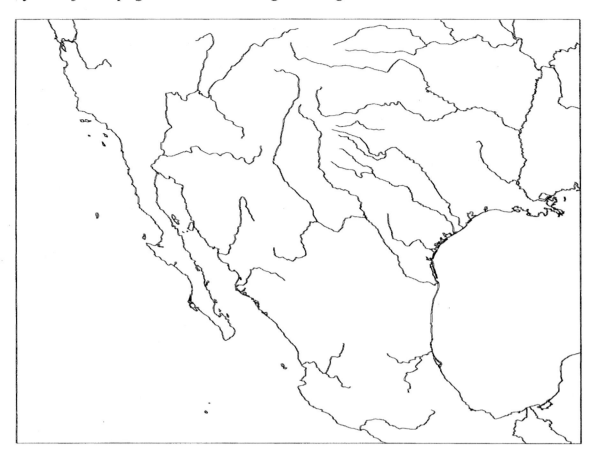

Interpreting the Past

Name _____ **Date** _____

Defend or refute the following statement: The Mexican-American War was an imperialist war.

DOCUMENT 1

The Treaties of Velasco (May 14, 1836)
Source: Texas State Historical Association, Texas History Links, Links to Some Texas History Primary Resource Documents on the Internet, compiled by Roger A. Griffin, Ph.D, Professor of History Emeritus, Austin Community College, Austin, Texas. http://home.austin.rr.com/rgriffin/texhisdocs.html

ARTICLES OF AGREEMENT AT SAN JACINTO

Whereas, The President Santa Anna, with divers officers of his late army, is a prisoner of war in charge of the army of Texas, and is desirous of terminating the contest now existing between the Government of Texas and that of Mexico, in which desire the Generals above named do fully concur, and Whereas, The President of the Republic of Texas, and the Cabinet, are also willing to stay the further effusion of blood, and to see the two neighboring Republics placed in relations of friendship, on terms of reciprocal advantage;

Therefore, it is agreed by the President Santa Anna, and the Generals Don Vicente Filisola, Don Jose Urea, Don Joaquin Ramires y Sesma, and Don Antonio Gaona...

5th. That the following be, and the same are hereby established and made the lines of demarcation between the two Republics of Mexico and of Texas, to wit: The line shall commence at the estuary or mouth of the Rio Grande, on the western bank thereof, and shall pursue the same bank up the said river, to the point where the river assumes the name of the Rio Bravo del Norte, from which point it shall proceed on the said western bank to the head waters, or source of said river, it being understood that the terms Rio Grande and Rio Bravo del Norte, apply to and designate one and the same stream. From the source of said river, the principal head branch being taken to ascertain that source, a due north line shall be run until it shall intersect the boundary line established and described in the Treaty negotiated by and between the Government of Spain and the Government of the United States of the North; which line was subsequently transferred to, and adopted in the Treaty of limits made between the Government of Mexico and that of the United States; and from this point of intersection the line shall be the same as was made and established in and by the several Treaties above mentioned, to continue to the mouth or outlet of the Sabine river, and from thence to the Gulf of Mexico.

DOCUMENT 2

Source: John L. O'Sullivan, "The Great Nation of Futurity" (1845)

America is destined for better deeds. It is our unparalleled glory that we have no reminiscences of battlefields, but in defense of humanity, of the oppressed of all nations, of the rights of conscience, the rights of personal enfranchisement. Our annals describe no scenes of horrid carnage, where men were led on by hundreds of thousands to slay one another, dupes and victims to emperors, kings, nobles, demons in the human form called heroes. We have had patriots to defend our homes, our liberties, but no aspirants to crowns or thrones; nor have the American people ever suffered themselves to be led on by wicked ambition to depopulate the land, to spread desolation far and wide, that a human being might be placed on a seat of supremacy.

DOCUMENT 3

Source: Thomas Corwin, Against the Mexican War (1847)

What is the territory, Mr. President, which you propose to wrest from Mexico? It is consecrated to the heart of the Mexican by many a well-fought battle with his old Castilian master. His Bunker Hills, and Saratogas, and Yorktowns are there! The Mexican can say, "There I bled for liberty! and shall I surrender that consecrated home of my affections to the Anglo-Saxon invaders? What do they want with it? They have Texas already. They have possessed themselves of the territory between the Nueces and the Rio Grande. What else do they want? To what shall I point my children as memorials of that independence which I bequeath to them, when those battlefields shall have passed from my possession?"

Sir, had one come and demanded Bunker Hill of the people of Massachusetts, had England's lion ever showed himself there, is there a man over thirteen and under ninety who would not have been ready to meet him? Is there a river on this continent that would not have run red with blood? Is there a field but would have been piled high with the unburied bones of slaughtered Americans before these consecrated battlefields of liberty should have been wrested from us? But this same American goes into a sister republic, and says to poor, weak Mexico, "Give up your territory, you are unworthy to possess it; I have got one half already, and all I ask of you is to give up the other!" ....

DOCUMENT 4

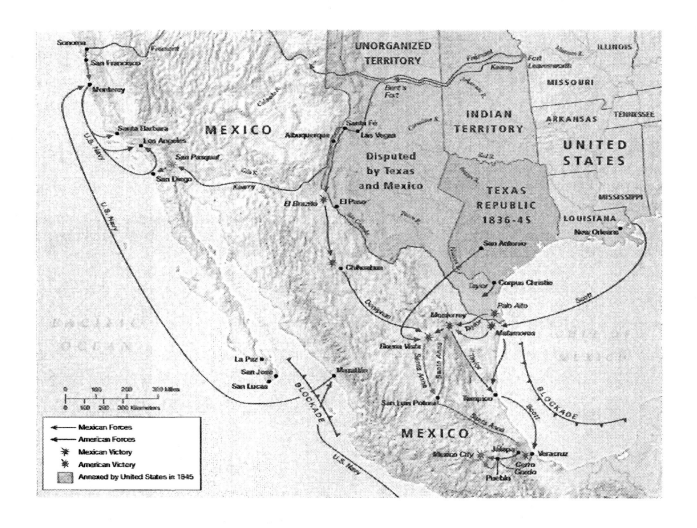

DOCUMENT 5

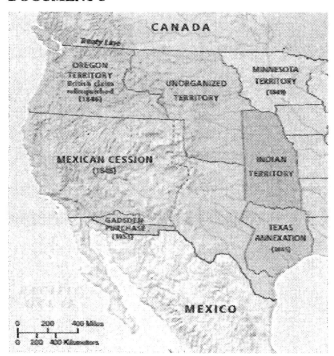

DOCUMENT 6

Source: President Polk Sends a Message to Congress

Mexico has passed the boundary of the United States, has invaded our territory and shed American blood upon American soil. . . . War exists, and, notwithstanding all our efforts to avoid it, exists by the act of Mexico herself.

DOCUMENT 7

DOCUMENT 8

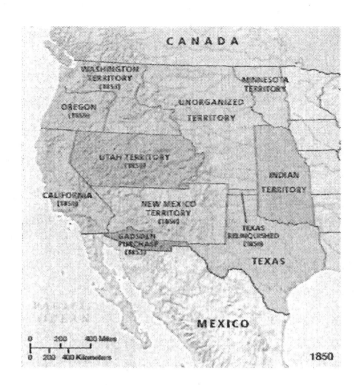

15. THE COMING CRISIS, THE 1850s

CHAPTER OVERVIEW

Summary

By 1850, the United States had made tremendous gains as a nation. The nineteenth century was a time of economic change and growth that created dynamic agricultural and manufacturing sectors within the country. The pursuit of manifest destiny had made the United States a continental nation with vast resources and land for its growing population to utilize. However, internal divisions over how those lands be developed created should hot debates and strident sectionalism. Northerners came to believe that the extension of slavery into new territories would deny average citizens equal access to success and contradicted the nation's commitment to freedom. For white Southerners, prohibiting slavery from new territories denied them equal rights within the nation and doomed to extinction the institution that they believed protected liberty. Political compromise, the longtime glue of the republic, failed to stem the tide of sectionalism as legislation like the Fugitive Slave and Kansas-Nebraska Acts actually increased hostility between the North and South. At times this hostility erupted into violence, as evidenced by Bleeding Kansas, the assault on Senator Sumner, and John Brown's raid on Harper's Ferry. When the national parties collapsed prior to the election of 1860, the Union's future was seriously compromised. Abraham Lincoln's victory in that race precipitated secession by Lower South states and made war seem inevitable.

Focus Questions

1. Why did people in the North and the South tend to see the issue of slavery so differently?

2. Why were the politicians of the 1850s unable to find a lasting political compromise on the issue of slavery?

3. What was the intent of the Compromise of 1850?

4. What explains the end of the Second American Party System and the rise of the Republican Party?

5. Why did the South secede following the Republican Party victory in the election of 1860?

CHAPTER REVIEW

Short Response: Consider these questions thoughtfully. Respond with the best possible short answer by filling in the blank.

1. In 1858 _____ and _____ publicly debated slavery as part of their pursuit of a seat in the Senate for the state of Illinois.

2. The most successful novel of the nineteenth century was _____ written by Harriet Beecher Stowe.

3. _____ of South Carolina was the principal spokesman for Southern interests since the Nullification Crisis of 1832.

4. Abolitionists warned the people of the North that their liberties were being threatened by a dark and menacing _____ emanating from the South.

5. The _____ in Congress prohibited the introduction of anti-slavery petitions on the floor of that body until 1844.

6. Proslavery advocates argued that Northern wage laborers were vulnerable to exploitation, starvation, and unemployment because they were trapped in _____.

7. The policy that allowed a territory acquired from Mexico to decide if it would or would not allow slavery to exist within its boundaries was _____.

8. In reaction to the Fugitive Slave Act, many Northern states passed _____ to prevent their citizens from having to participate in the capture of runaway slaves.

9. The 1854 capture of runaway slave _____ created a wave of anger and protests against the enforcement of the Fugitive Slave Act in Massachusetts.

10. The _____ was a bungled effort by the Pierce administration to acquire the Spanish colony of Cuba in 1854.

Multiple Choice: Select the response that best answers each question or best completes each sentence.

1. The significance of the Lincoln/Douglas Debates of 1858:
    a. was that Abraham Lincoln gained a national reputation and that the Republican Party represented the only political party that was able or willing to stop the expansion of slavery.
    b. was that the two leaders reached an agreement in regard to slavery in the territories.
    c. was that Lincoln's victory elevated him to a position in the Senate from which he could launch his presidential aspirations.
    d. was that it was here that Lincoln first publicly declared his belief in racial equality.

2. During the 1830s and 1840s all of the following Christian denominations split along regional lines except the:
    a. Presbyterians.
    b. Catholics.
    c. Methodists.
    d. Baptists.

3. The Compromise of 1850 included each of the following measures except:
    a. Fugitive Slave Act.
    b. the end of the domestic slave trade in Washington.
    c. the admission of California as a state with popular sovereignty.
    d. a reduction in the borders of Texas.

4. The law passed in 1850 that generated widespread emotional opposition in the North was:
   a. the new fugitive slave law.
   b. the admission of California as a free state.
   c. the establishment of the modern border of Texas.
   d. the outlawing of the slave trade in Washington, D.C.

5. According to abolitionists, the Slave Power:
   a. denied many people throughout the United States the right to free speech.
   b. illegally censored the mail.
   c. deprived poor whites of their democratic rights.
   d. all of the above.

6. The federal legislation that pushed the national party system into crisis was:
   a. the Dawes Severalty Act.
   b. the Compromise of 1850.
   c. the Kansas-Nebraska Act.
   d. the Gadsden Purchase Act.

7. William Walker was a young filibuster who tried to acquire new slave territory for the United States by invading which of the following Central American nations three times:
   a. Costa Rica.
   b. Nicaragua.
   c. Belize.
   d. Guatemala.

8. Nativist politics in the 1850s were shaped by the:
   a. America Firsters.
   b. Amerian Indian Party.
   c. Know Nothings.
   d. Democratic Party.

9. The passage of the Kansas-Nebraska Act led the creation of which political party:
   a. Republicans.
   b. Whigs.
   c. Democrats.
   d. Free Soil Party.

10. In the Dred Scott decision, Chief Justice Roger Taney:
    a. restored the Missouri Compromise line that had been overturned by the Kansas-Nebraska Act.
    b. declared that African Americans were not citizens of the United States and had no legal rights.
    c. wrote that only Congress had the authority to prohibit the expansion of slavery into new territories.
    d. announced that slaves who had lived in a free territory had to be emancipated with all due haste.

11. Bleeding Kansas:
    a. was the name given to the US Senator from that state who was beaten in the Senate chambers.
    b. refers to the open warfare that raged in that territory following the passage of the Kansas-Nebraska Act.
    c. describes the second eviction suffered by Indian tribes once white settlers moved into Kansas.
    d. is a poem by Walt Whitman describing the murder of proslavery settlers in Kansas.

12. The dramatic event that helped further polarize the nation in 1859 was:
    a. the publication of the novel *Uncle Tom's Cabin*.
    b. an attack on free-soil settlers at Osowatomie Creek.

c. the firing on Fort Sumter by the South Carolina militia.

d. John Brown's raid on the arsenal at Harper's Ferry.

13. For many Southerners, the Panic of 1857:
    a. shook their faith in the dependability of slave labor.
    b. confirmed their commitment to King Cotton and slavery.
    c. made many worry about the superiority of the North's economy to their own.
    d. was the last straw that led them to seek independence.

14. In the election of 1860:
    a. the Republican Party retained its traditional hold on the South.
    b. Lincoln carried only three of the Lower South states.
    c. Lincoln won a decisive victory in the electoral college.
    d. Republicans narrowly defeated a united Democratic Party.

15. All of the above were features of the Republican platform in 1860 except:
    a. a strong condemnation of John Brown assault on Harper's Ferry.
    b. a statement denying social equality between the races.
    c. an acceptance of popular sovereignty in all western territories.
    d. support for a homestead act.

Thought Questions: Think carefully about the following questions or comments. Your answers should prepare you to participate in class discussions or help you to write an effective essay. In both class discussions and essays you should always support the arguments you make by referring to specific examples and historical evidence. You may use the space provided to sketch out ideas or outline your response.

1. How did the territorial expansion that occurred prior to 1850 help define politics, culture, and national or sectional identity in the United States?

2. Describe the five legislative bills that became the Compromise of 1850. Many at the time believed this compromise saved the union. Why were they mistaken about this agreement's ability to maintain the Union and peace?

3. Discuss the significance of the Kansas-Nebraska Act? How did this legislation and the events in Kansas which followed it, influence the American political system?

4. How did the *Dred Scott* decision, the LeCompton Constitution, the Panic of 1857, and John Brown's Raid add to the turmoil of the late 1850s?

5. Discuss the election of 1860. Who ran and what were the central ideas of their candidacy? How did the South react to the Republican victory?

Map Skills: These questions are based on the maps in the chapter. Please use the blank map provided here for your answers.

1. Identify the geographical implications of popular sovereignty as reflected in the Compromise of 1850 and the Kansas-Nebraska Act of 1854.

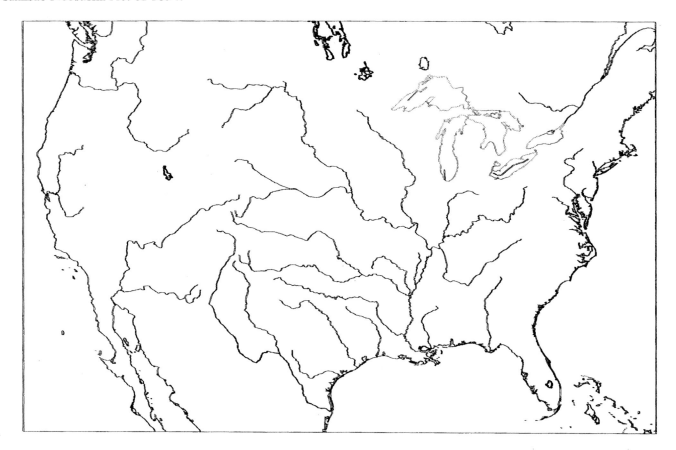

2. Compare the results of the elections of 1856 and 1860. What areas voted for each candidate? What are some noticeable differences between the two elections?

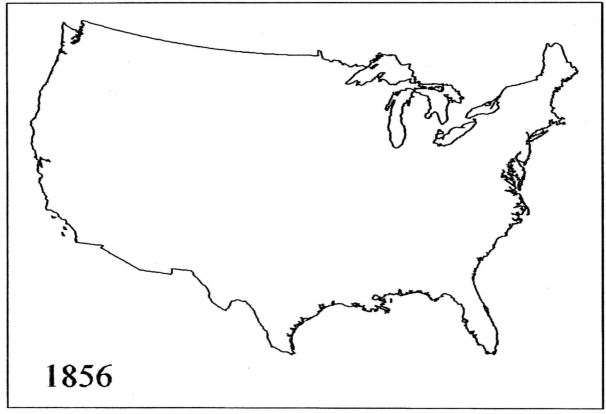

1856

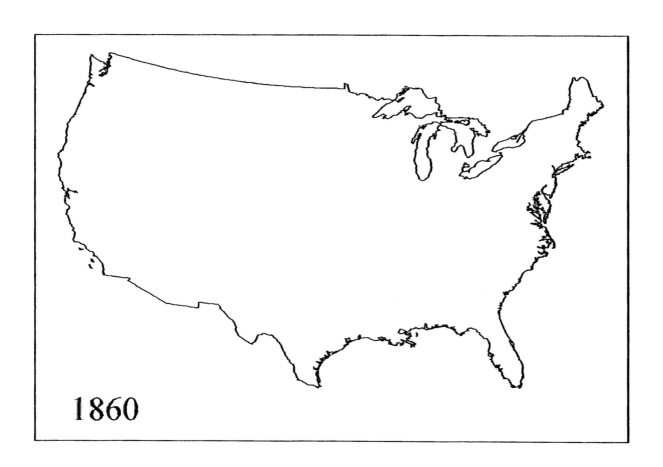

1860

3. Locate the seven states that originally seceded from the Union. Identify the additional states that joined the Confederacy. Which states were the border states?

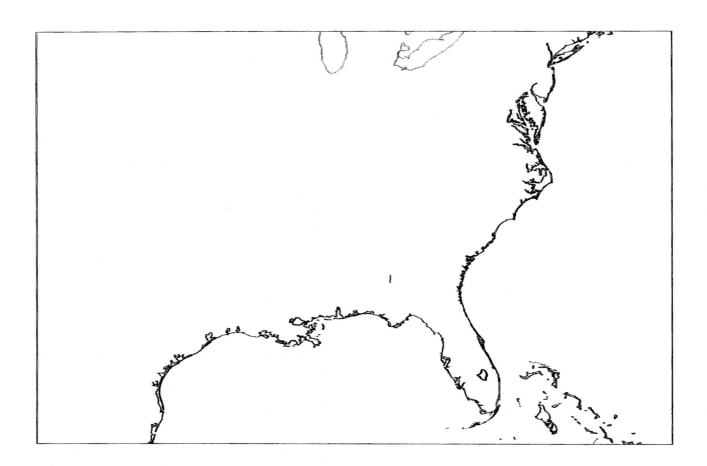

Interpreting the Past

Name _____ Date _____

> The ultimate "cause" of the Civil War has been a matter of intense debate among historians. Evaluate the various factors contributing to the outbreak of war and determine which was the most significant and why.

DOCUMENT 1
Source: William Lloyd Garrison, from The Liberator (1831)

Assenting to the "self-evident truth" maintained in the American Declaration of Independence "that all men are created equal, and endowed by their Creator with certain inalienable rights-among which are life, liberty, and the pursuit of happiness," I shall strenuously contend for the immediate enfranchisement of our slave population. . . . In Park Street Church, on the Fourth of July, 1829, in an address on slavery, I unreflectingly assented to the popular but pernicious doctrine of gradual abolition. I seize this opportunity to make a full and unequivocal recantation, and thus publicly to ask pardon of my God, of my country, and of my brethren the poor slaves, for having uttered a sentiment so full of timidity, injustice, and absurdity. . . .

I am aware that many object to the severity of my language; but is there not cause for severity? I will be as harsh as truth, and as uncompromising as justice. On this subject I do not wish to think, or speak, or write, with moderation. No! No! Tell a man whose house is on fire to give a moderate alarm; tell him to moderately rescue his wife from the hands of the ravisher; tell the mother to gradually extricate her babe from the fire into which it has fallen-but urge me not to use moderation in a cause like the present. I am in earnest-will not equivocate-I will not excuse-I will not retreat in a single inch-and I will be heard.

DOCUMENT 2
Source: Harriet Beecher Stowe, from Uncle Tom's Cabin (1852)

"Well, here's a pious dog, at last, let down among us sinners-a saint, a gentleman, and no less, to talk to us sinners about our sins! Powerful holy crittur, he must be! Here, you rascal, you make believe to be so pious-didn't you never hear, out of yer Bible, 'Servants, obey yer masters'? An't I yer master? Didn't I pay down twelve hundred dollars, cash, for all there is inside yer old cussed black shell? An't yer mine, now, body and soul?" he said, giving Tom a violent kick with his heavy boot; "tell me!"

In the very depth of physical suffering, bowed by brutal oppression, this question shot a gleam of joy and triumph through Tom's soul. He suddenly stretched himself up, and, looking earnestly to heaven, while the tears and blood that flowed down his face mingled, he exclaimed, " No! no! no! my soul an't yours, Mas'r! You haven't bought it-ye can't buy it! It's been bought and paid for by One that is able to keep it. No matter, no matter, you can't harm me!"

"I can't!" said Legree, with a sneer; "we'll see-we'll see! Here Sambo, Quimbo, give this dog such a breakin' in as he won't get over this month!"

DOCUMENT 3

A Dying Statesman Speaks Out Against the Compromise of 1850
Source: The Library of Congress, American Memory: Historical Collections for the National Digital Library
http://lcweb2.loc.gov/cgi-bin/query/r?ammem/mcc:@field(DOCID+@lit(mcc/009))

The result of the whole of these causes combined is that the North has acquired a decided ascendancy over every department of this government, and through it a control over all the powers of the system. A single section, governed by the will of the numerical majority, has now in fact the control of the government and the entire powers of the system. What was once a constitutional federal republic is now converted, in reality, into one as absolute as that of the Autocrat of Russia, and as despotic in its tendency as any absolute government that ever existed.

As, then, the North has the absolute control over the government, it is manifest that on all questions between it and the South, where there is a diversity of interests, the interests of the latter will be sacrificed to the former, however oppressive the effects may be, as the South possesses no means by which it can resist through the action of the government. But if there was no question of vital importance to the South, in reference to which there was a diversity of views between the two sections, this state of things might be endured without the hazard of destruction to the South. There is a question of vital importance to the Southern section, in reference to which the views and feelings of the two sections are as opposite and hostile as they can possibly be.

I refer to the relation between the two races in the Southern section, which constitutes a vital portion of her social organization. Every portion of the North entertains views and feelings more or less hostile to it. Those most opposed and hostile regard it a sin, and consider themselves under most sacred obligation to use every effort to destroy it. Indeed, to the extent that they conceive they have power, they regard themselves as implicated in the sin and responsible for suppressing it by the use of all and every means. Those less opposed and hostile regard it as a crime—an offense against humanity, as they call it—and, although not so fanatical, feel themselves bound to use all efforts to effect the same object; while those who are least opposed and hostile regard it as a blot and a stain on the character of what they call the nation, and feel themselves accordingly bound to give it no countenance or support. On the contrary, the Southern section regards the relation as one which cannot be destroyed without subjecting the two races to the greatest calamity and the section to poverty, desolation, and wretchedness; and accordingly they feel bound by every consideration of interest and safety to defend it.

This hostile feeling on the part of the North toward the social organization of the South long lay dormant, but it only required some cause to act on those who felt most intensely that they were responsible for its continuance to call it into action. The increasing power of this government and of the control of the Northern section over all its departments furnished the cause. It was this which made an impression on the minds of many that there was little or no restraint to prevent the government from doing whatever it might choose to do. This was sufficient of itself to put the most fanatical portion of the North in action for the purpose of destroying the existing relation between the two races in the South.

DOCUMENT 4

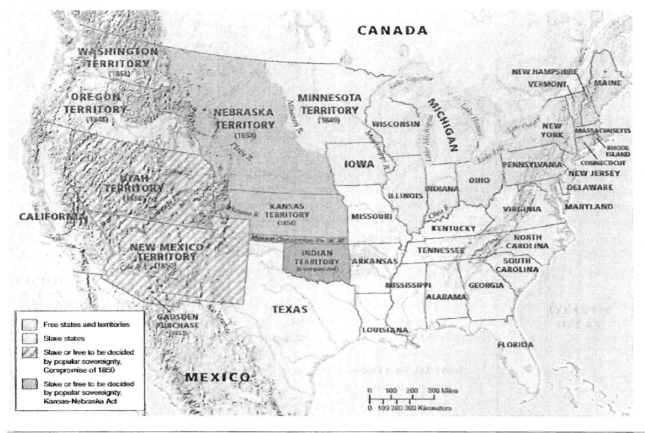

DOCUMENT 5

BATTLE OF HICKORY POINT, 20 MILES NORTH OF LAWRENCE

DOCUMENT 6

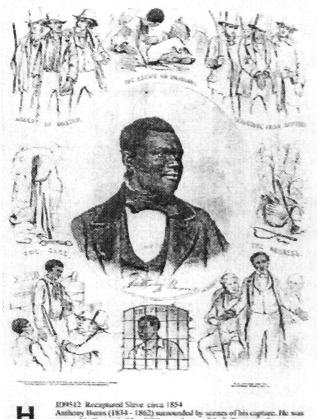

H JD952 Recaptured Slave circa 1854
Anthony Burns (1834 - 1862) surrounded by scenes of his capture. He was
arrested in Boston in May 1854 on a charge of theft. Recognized as a
fugitive slave, his return to Virginia was the cause of riots. After he was
bought out of slavery, he later became pastor of a Negro baptist church in
St. Catherine's Canada.
PHOTO: HULTON GETTY / LIAISON AGENCY

DOCUMENT 7
Source: Dred Scott v. Sanford (1857)

The Question is simply this: Can a negro, whose ancestors were imported into this country, and sold as slaves, become a member of the political community formed and brought into existence by the Constitution of the United States, and as such become entitled to all the rights, and privileges, and immunities, guarantied [sic] by that instrument to the citizen? One of which rights is the privilege of suing in a court of the United States in the cases specified in the constitution.

. . . The only matter in issue before the Court, therefore, is, whether the descendants of such slaves, when they shall be emancipated, or who are born of parents who had become free before their birth, are citizens of a State, in the sense which the word citizen is used in the Constitution. . . .

The words "people of the United States" and "citizens" are synonymous terms. . . . They both describe the political body who, according to our republican institutions, form the sovereignty, and who hold the power and conduct the government through their representatives. . . . The question before us is, whether the class of persons described in the plea in abatement compose a portion of this people, and are constituent members of this sovereignty? We think they are not, under the word "citizens" in the Constitution, and can therefore claim none of the rights and privileges which that instrument provides for and secures to citizens of the United States. On the contrary, they were at that time considered as a subordinate and inferior class of beings, who had been subjugated by the dominant race, and whether emancipated or not, yet remained subject to their authority, and had no rights or privileges but such as those who held the power and the government might choose to grant them. . . .

In discussing the question, we must not confound the rights of citizenship which a State may confer within its own limits, and the rights of citizenship as a member of the Union. It does not by any means follow, because he has all the rights and privileges of a citizen of a State, that he must be a citizen of the United States. . . .

In the opinion of the court, the legislation and histories of the times, and the language used in the Declaration of Independence, show, that neither the class of persons who had been imported as slaves, nor their descendants, whether they had become free or not, were then acknowledged as a part of the people, nor intended to be included in the general words used in that memorable instrument. . . .

They had for more than a century before been regarded as beings of an inferior order, and altogether unfit to associate with the white race, either in social or political relations, and so far inferior, that they had no rights which the white man was bound to respect; and that the negro might justly and lawfully be reduced to slavery for his benefit. . . .

. . . there are two clauses in the constitution which point directly and specifically to the negro race as a separate class of persons, and show clearly that they were not regarded as a portion of the people or citizens of the government then formed.

. . . upon full and careful consideration of the subject, the court is of opinion, that, upon the facts stated. . . Dred Scott was not a citizen of Missouri within the meaning of the constitution of the United States and not entitled as such to sue in its courts. . . .

DOCUMENT 8

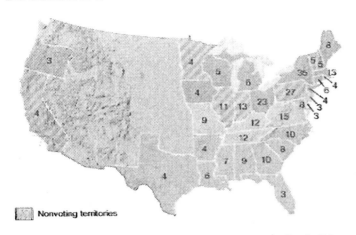

	Electoral Vote (%)	Popular Vote (%)
ABRAHAM LINCOLN (Republican)	180 (59)	1,865,593 (40)
John C. Breckinridge (Southern Democrat)	72 (24)	848,356 (18)
John Bell (Constitutional Union)	39 (13)	592,906 (13)
Stephen A. Douglas (Northern Democrat)	12 (4)	1,382,713 (29)
States that Republicans lost in 1856, won in 1860		

Nonvoting territories

DOCUMENT 9
Abraham Lincoln, "A House Divided" (1858)

If we could first know where we are, and whither we are tending, we could better judge what to do and how to do it. We are now far into the fifth year since a policy was initiated with the avowed object, and confident promise, of putting an end to slavery agitation. Under the operation of that policy, that agitation has not only not ceased but has constantly augmented. In my opinion, it will not cease until a crisis shall have been reached and passed. "A house divided against itself cannot stand." I believe this government cannot endure permanently half-slave and half-free. I do not expect the Union to be dissolved-I do not expect the house to fall-but I do expect it will cease to be divided. It will become all one thing or all the other. Either the opponents of slavery will arrest the further spread of it and place it where the public mind shall rest in the belief that it is in the course of ultimate extinction or its advocates will push it forward, till it shall become alike lawful in all the states, old as well as new-North as well as South.

16. THE CIVIL WAR, 1861–1865

CHAPTER OVERVIEW

Summary

The 1860 election of Abraham Lincoln led most of the slaveholding states to secede from the Union and attempt to establish a new nation. In the war that followed, more than 600,000 Americans would be killed in the successful effort to preserve the Union. When the Union was saved, slavery was destroyed and several million African Americans finally were freed from bondage. Union victory resulted from superior advantages in men, material, and the dogged determination of the commander-in-chief and his handpicked generals. However, the war was longer and bloodier than either side anticipated, and both the Confederacy and Union had to confront internal divisions over wartime policy. These divisions often reflected longstanding antipathies related to class, race, sex, and political ideology. Only time would tell if the victorious powers could minimize such discontent as it tried to rebuild the nation anew.

Focus Questions

1. What advantages did the North possess at the outset of the Civil War?

2. How did the power of the federal government expand as the war progressed?

3. What successes did the South enjoy in the early years of the war?

4. How did the end of slavery affect the war efforts of the North and South?

5. What impact did the war have on northern political, economic, and social life? and on the same aspects of southern life?

6. How did Grant and Sherman exemplify a new war strategy?

CHAPTER REVIEW

Short Response: Consider these questions thoughtfully. Respond with the best possible short answer by filling in the blank.

1. The Illinois "botanic physician" also known as the Cyclone in Calico who worked to immune the health of Union soldiers was _____.

2. The first shots of the Civil War were fired at _____ in the state of South Carolina.

3. When Union soldiers from Massachusetts marched into the border state city of _____ they were greeted by a pro-Confederate mob who pelted them with bricks.

4. The death toll among soldiers in the Civil War was _____.

5. The President of the newly formed Confederate States of America was _____.

6. The _____ was passed in 1862 and created the first national currency in the United States.

7. A key feature of the Confederacy's foreign relations was its belief that _____ would force nations like Britain to recognize it as an independent nation.

8. When enlistments fell off in 1862, the _____ instituted the first military draft in American history.

9. General _____ was a timid Union field commander whose repeated failure to vigorously prosecute war against the Army of Northern Virginia forced Lincoln to remove him from command.

10. The city of _____ was considered the "Gibraltar of the Mississippi" and became a major target of General Grant in the Western theater of the Civil War.

Multiple Choice: Select the response that best answers each question or best completes each sentence.

1. Which of the following accurately identifies the slaveholding border states that did not secede:
   a. Arkansas, Missouri, Kentucky, Delaware.
   b. Virginia, Missouri, Arkansas, Maryland.
   c. Delaware, Missouri, Arkansas, Virginia.
   d. Maryland, Delaware, Kentucky, Missouri.

2. When President Lincoln called for volunteers following the surrender of Fort Sumter:
   a. very few men came forward to join in what they viewed as an unnecessary war.
   b. the Union army enlisted virtually every free African American who volunteered.
   c. New Englanders responded enthusiastically but other northerners did not.
   d. four additional slave states declared secession and joined the Confederacy.

3. During which early Civil War battle did onlookers follow the Union Army to the field to watch the day's events?:
   a. Shiloh.
   b. Antietam.
   c. Fana's Crossroads.
   d. Bull Run.

4. During the Civil War the Union benefited from all of the following advantages except:
   a. number of soldiers in the field.
   b. amount and quality of railroad mileage.
   c. fighting a primarily defensive war.
   d. greater industrial capacity.

5. One result of national war-time policies was:
   a. the issuance of a national currency known as "Greenbacks."
   b. the incorporation of dozens of state banks to issue bank notes.
   c. the determination by the government that all money had to be specie.
   d. the decentralization of the banking industry to keep state banks solvent.

6. King Cotton Diplomacy:
   a. was the Union's all-out war effort to destroy all of the South's cotton-producing capability.
   b. allowed the Confederacy to earn millions of dollars to finance its conduct of the Civil War.
   c. was successful until 1864 when the Union blockade finally cut off southern commerce.
   d. was the basis for the South's mistaken belief that England would recognize the Confederacy.

7. The phrase "a rich man's war and a poor man's fight":
   a. was heard as soon as the Union became the first to pass a conscription law.
   b. did not apply to the Civil War as all people shared the burden of war evenly.
   c. reflected the Confederacy's exemption of one white man from military service for each 20 slaves owned.
   d. was a reflection of the unity that white Southerners felt about the war.

8. The Emancipation Proclamation:
   a. was issued when the war began in order to be able to enlist former slaves into the federal army.
   b. freed all slaves within the United States.
   c. was issued after Grant's victory at Vicksburg.
   d. freed all slaves held in areas in rebellion against the United States.

9. During the Civil War:

a. African Americans served as combat troops for the first time in U.S. history.

b. northern racism prevented any African Americans from serving as combat troops.

c. African Americans and women served in a variety of capacities for the Union forces.

d. southern prejudice meant that slaves could not work on the Confederate war effort.

10. All of the following were reasons for the high casualty rates of the Civil War except:
    a. disease and medical ignorance.
    b. improved firearm accuracy.
    c. the legacy of the Jomini Doctrine.
    d. George McClellan's relentlessly aggressive tactics.

11. During the Civil war:
    a. most Northerners protested against conscription laws because they believed the war was immoral and should end quickly.
    b. Northern resistance to conscription revealed that there were deep class resentments and sharp racial differences in the Union.
    c. Copperheads were among the most faithful supporters of Lincoln.
    d. the New York Draft Riots were so successful that they led to a sharp drop in the number of people who supported the war.

12. At the beginning of the Civil War many opposed women working as military nurses:
    a. because women are too squeamish for such work.
    b. since caring for men outside of one's family was deemed unseemly for respectable women.
    c. since women's wages were too high for the government to pay at a time of war.
    d. because so few dependable women could be found.

13. Key victories for the Union in 1863 came at:
    a. Antietam and Shiloh.
    b. Fredericksburg and Chancellorsville.
    c. Vicksburg and Gettysburg.
    d. Concord and Lexington.

14. William Tecumseh Sherman's Special Field Order #15:
    a. was an attempt to stop his soldiers from abusing Southerners and their property.
    b. granted freed African Americans 40 acre farms from a designated area of 400,000 acres.
    c. commanded soldiers in his command to burn every house they encountered.
    d. was overturned by Lincoln for being unconstitutional.

15. The 1864 election:
    a. guaranteed that Lincoln's policy of unconditional surrender would continue.
    b. gave the Confederacy hope that peace negotiations might happen.
    c. saw most Union soldiers vote against Lincoln.
    d. was of no interest to the Confederates since they had already left the Union.

Thought Questions: Think carefully about the following questions or comments. Your answers should prepare you to participate in class discussions or help you to write an effective essay. In both class discussions and essays you should always support the arguments you make by referring to specific examples and historical evidence. You may use the space provided to sketch out ideas or outline your response.

1. Describe how the events of 1861 led to war and how that war developed in the early months of the conflict. Discuss the various advantages and disadvantages each side faced as the war began.

2. How would you describe the results of the war prior to 1863? How was the South proving successful? In what ways was the North gaining an advantage?

3. Describe how the Emancipation Proclamation was a response to the war situation Abraham Lincoln faced. What were the results of the proclamation?

4. Discuss how the war turned in favor of the Union in 1863, and how the federal forces took advantage of that in 1864 and 1865.

5. How did women and African Americans participate in the Civil War? What were some of the obstacles that both of these groups had to overcome before they were allowed to serve?

Map Skills: These questions are based on the maps in the chapter. Please use the blank map provided here for your answers.

1. What areas of the Confederacy did Union forces occupy in 1861 and 1862; in 1863; in 1864 and 1865? How did those territorial gains reflect the evolving federal strategy for the war?

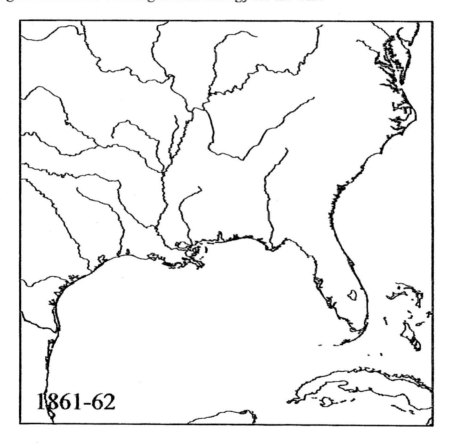

1861-62

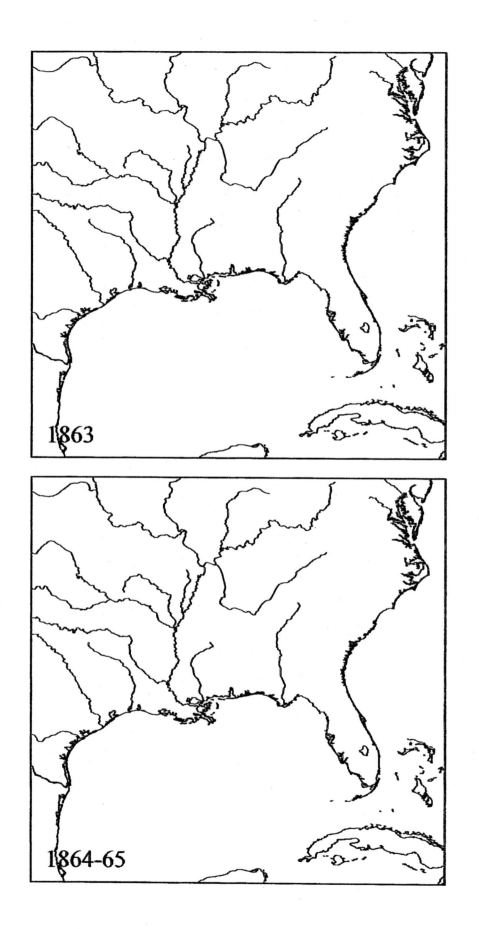

1863

1864-65

2. Locate the major battles that were fought in the eastern theater of operations and in the western theater of operations.

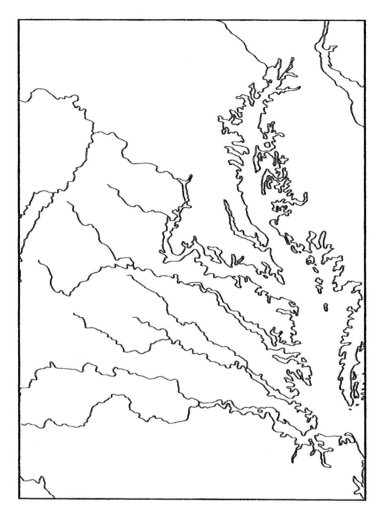

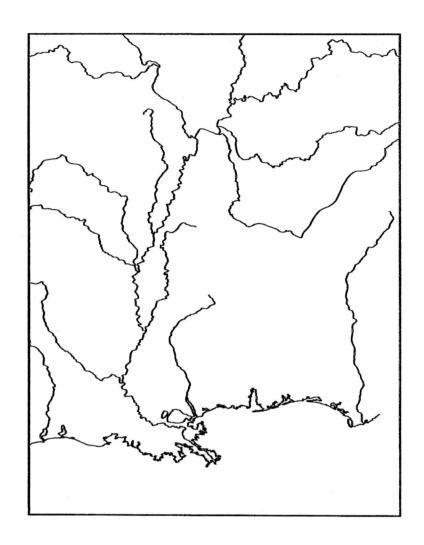

Interpreting the Past

Name _____ Date _____

Describe some of the justifications that Confederates used for secession and for their loyalty to the Confederacy over the Union.

DOCUMENT 1

Source: Jefferson Davis, Address to the Provisional Congress of the Confederate
States of America (1861)

The declaration of war made against this Confederacy by Abraham Lincoln, the President of the United States, in his proclamation issued on the 15th day of the present month, rendered it necessary, in my judgment, that you should convene at the earliest practicable moment to devise the measures necessary for the defense of the country. The occasion is indeed an extraordinary one. It justifies me in a brief review of the relations heretofore existing between us and the States which now unite in warfare against us and in a succinct statement of the events which have resulted in this warfare, to the end that mankind may pass intelligent and impartial judgment on its motives and objects. During the war waged against Great Britain by her colonies on this continent a common danger impelled them to a close alliance and to the formation of a Confederation, by the terms of which the colonies, styling themselves States, entered "*severally* into a firm league of friendship with each other for their common defense, the security of their liberties, and their mutual and general welfare, binding themselves to assist each other against all force offered to or attacks made upon them, or any of them, on account of religion, sovereignty, trade, or any other pretense whatever." In order to guard against any misconstruction of their compact, the several States made explicit declaration in a distinct article-that "*each* State *retains its* sovereignty, freedom, and independence, and every power, jurisdiction, and right which is not by this Confederation *expressly delegated* to the United States in Congress assembled." . . .

DOCUMENT 2

The "Cornerstone Speech" (1861)
Source: Henry Cleveland, Alexander H. Stephens, in Public and Private: With Letters and Speeches, Before, During, and Since the War, Philadelphia, 1886, pp. 717–729.
http://www.geocities.com/CollegePark/Quad/6460/doct/861crnrstn.html

Our new government is founded upon exactly the opposite idea; its foundations are laid, its corner-stone rests upon the great truth, that the negro is not equal to the white man; that slavery—subordination to the superior race—is his natural and normal condition. [Applause.] This, our new government, is the first, in the history of the world, based upon this great physical, philosophical, and moral truth. This truth has been slow in the process of its development, like all other truths in the various departments of science. It has been so even amongst us. Many who hear me, perhaps, can recollect well, that this truth was not generally admitted, even within their day. The errors of the past generation still clung to many as late as twenty years ago. Those at the North, who still cling to these errors, with a zeal above knowledge, we justly denominate fanatics. All fanaticism springs from an aberration of the mind—from a defect in reasoning. It is a species of insanity. One of the most striking characteristics of insanity, in many instances, is forming correct conclusions from fancied or erroneous premises; so with the anti-slavery fanatics; their conclusions are right if their premises were. They assume that the negro is equal, and hence conclude that he is entitled to equal privileges and rights with the white man. If their premises were correct, their conclusions would be logical and just—but their premise being wrong, their whole argument fails. I recollect once of having heard a gentleman from one of the northern States, of great power and ability, announce in the House of Representatives, with imposing effect, that we of the South would be compelled, ultimately, to yield upon this subject of slavery, that it was as impossible to war successfully against a principle in politics, as it was in physics or mechanics. That the principle would ultimately prevail. That we, in maintaining slavery as it exists with us, were warring against a principle, a principle founded in nature, the principle of the equality of men. The reply I made to him was, that upon his own grounds, we should, ultimately, succeed, and that he and his associates, in this crusade against our institutions, would ultimately fail. The truth announced, that it was as impossible to war successfully against a principle in politics as it was in physics and mechanics, I admitted; but told him that it was he, and those acting with him, who were warring against a principle. They were attempting to make things equal which the Creator had made unequal.

DOCUMENT 3

Why They Fought (1861)
Source: George Edward Pickett, The Heart of a Soldier, As Revealed in the Intimate Letters of Genl. George E. Pickett
C.S.A.: Electronic Edition.
http://docsouth.unc.edu/pickett/pickett.html#pick33

You know, my little lady, some of those cross-stitched mottoes on the cardboard samplers which used to hang on my nursery wall, such as, "He who provides not for his own household is worse than an infidel" and "Charity begins at home," made a lasting impression upon me; and while I love my neighbor, i.e., my country, I love my household, i.e., my state, more, and I could not be an infidel and lift my sword against my own kith and kin, even though I do believe, my most wise little counselor and confidante, that the measure of American greatness can be achieved only under one flag, and I fear, alas, there can never again reign for either of us the true spirit of national unity whether divided under two flags or united under one...
Now, little one, if you had the very faintest idea how happy a certain captain in the C.S.A. (My, but that "C" looks queer!) would be to look into your beautiful, soul-speaking eyes and hear your wonderfully musical voice, I think you would let him know by wire where he could find you. I shall almost listen for the electricity which says, "I am at —. Come." I know that you will have mercy on your devoted SOLDIER.

DOCUMENT 4

DOCUMENT 5

Source: Mary Boykin Chesnut, A Confederate Lady's Diary (1861)

I wonder if it be a sin to think slavery a curse to any land. Sumner said not one word of this hated institution which is not true. Men & women are punished when their masters & mistresses are brutes & not when they do wrong-& then we live surrounded by prostitutes. An abandoned woman is sent out of any decent house elsewhere. Who thinks any worse of a Negro or Mulatto woman for being a thing we can't name. God forgive us, but ours is a monstrous system & wrong & iniquity. Perhaps the rest of the world is as bad. This is only what I see: like the patriarchs of old, our men live all in one house with their wives & their concubines, & the Mulattos one sees in every family exactly resemble the white children-& every lady tells you who is the father of all the Mulatto children in everybody's household, but those in her own, she seems to think drop from the clouds or pretends so to think-. Good women we have, but they talk of nastiness tho they never do wrong; they talk day & night of -. My disgust sometimes is boiling over-but they are, I believe, in conduct the purest women God ever made. Thank God for my countrywomen-alas for the men! No worse than men everywhere, but the lower their mistresses, the more degraded they must be.

DOCUMENT 6

Source: Charles Harvey Brewster, Three Letters from the Civil War Front (1862)

I don't know but I shall be discharged, as the whole Regiment is almost in a state of mutiny on the Nigger question. Capt Miller the pro slavery Captain of the Shelburne Falls Co undertook with Major Marsh to back him to drive all the Contraband out of camp, he came to me and I had quite a blow up with him. Major Marsh took the Regiment off the camp to drill yesterday while they were gone Capt Miller searched the camp for niggers, but did not find any, this morning they are all here again, this morning placards were found posted around the camp threatening direful things if they persisted in driving them off, which is a most foolish thing, but the men did not come down here to oppress Niggers and they are not quite brutes yet, as some of their officers are. I have nothing to do with any of the trouble except that I refuse to order off my own servant, in this I am not alone, as Capt Walkly of the Westfield Co has done the same thing, the Officers are divided into two parties on the question, and most bitter and rancorous feelings have been excited which will never be allayed. I do not know how it will all end but I should not be all surprised if they made a fuss about it and should prefer charges against me, Capt Parsons, Lieut Weatherill, the Adjutant, Capt Walkley, Capt Lombard, Lieut Shurtleff, + our one or two others hold the same opinion that I do in the matter. I should hate to have to leave now just as the Regiment is going into active service, but I never will be instrumental in returning a slave to his master in any way shape or manner, I'll die first. Major Marsh well knows that the slaves masters are waiting outside of camp ready to snap them up, and it is inhuman to drive them into their hands, if you could have seen strong men crying like children, at the very thought as I did yesterday you would not blame me for standing out about it nor can one blame the men for showing sympathy for them, for they are from Massachusetts and are entirely unused to such scenes, and cannot recognize this property in human flesh and blood.

DOCUMENT 7

Source: John Dooley, Passages from a Journal (1863)

I tell you, there is no romance in making one of these charges. You might think so from reading 'Charlies O'Malley,' that prodigy of valour, or in reading of any other gallant knight who would as little think of riding over gunners and such like as they would of eating a dozen oysters. But when you rise to your feet as we did today, I tell you the enthusiasm of ardent breasts in many cases ain't there, and instead of burning to avenge the insults of our country, families and altars and firesides, and the thought is most frequently, Oh. if I could just come out of this charge safely how thankful would I be!

17. RECONSTRUCTION, 1863–1877

CHAPTER OVERVIEW

Summary

When the Civil War ended, the nation faced the enormous task of how to put the two rival sections back together again. Further complicating that challenge was the clear need to determine the role that newly-freed African Americans would play in the nation. After the assassination of Abraham Lincoln, the responsibility for crafting workable policies in these areas fell to President Andrew Johnson and the Congress, neither of which could find a way to agree with the other. The resultant feud led to the creation of rival reconstruction policies and the nation's first impeachment proceeding against a sitting President. Caught in the crossfire of an angry white Southern population and squabbling or short sighted policymakers, were the former slaves. Despite facing violence and intimidation throughout the period, African Americans strove to restore and protect their families, gain literacy, and establish their own institutions. While making enormous strides in these areas and gaining significant new liberties, they struggled to gain economic independence as Congressional leaders could not bring themselves to provide the freed men land. In the wake of this failure, sharecropping, tenant-farming, and the crop lien became the fate of most former slaves, as well as a significant percentage of the South's white farmers. When the United States' economy struggled in the 1870s and worker/employer violence erupted, the nation's focus shifted away from the South and Reconstruction. As a result, many of the goals and promises of Reconstruction would remain unfulfilled until the coming of the Civil Rights Movement nearly a century later.

Focus Questions

1. What were the competing political plans for reconstructing the defeated Confederacy?

2. How did African Americans negotiate the difficult transition from slavery to freedom?

3. What were the most important political and social legacies of Reconstruction in the southern states?

4. How did economic and political transformations in the North reflect another side of Reconstruction?

CHAPTER REVIEW

Short Response: Consider these questions thoughtfully. Respond with the best possible short answer by filling in the blank.

1. The _____ was a body that functioned as the organizational arm of the Republican Party in the Reconstruction South.

2. The _____ was a secretive terrorist organization that intimidated, injured, and murdered black and white Republicans in the South during Reconstruction.

3. The _____ was ratified during Reconstruction and granted African Americans citizenship rights in the United States.

4. The _____ was the federal government's attempt to stop organized terrorist violence in the South.

5. The famous African American call for _____ probably emanated from Sherman's Special Field Order #15.

6. _____ was the former Tennessee senator who became President after the assassination of Abraham Lincoln.

7. The _____ were laws passed by Southern governments in the first year after the war which attempted to restrict the new found freedom of the region's former slaves.

8. One of the central arguments Congress used to impeach President Johnson was his supposed violation of the _____ Act.

9. The _____ guaranteed African American men the right to vote.

10. By the late 1860s _____ and _____ became the most common modes of agricultural organization and production in the South.

Multiple Choice: Select the response that best answers each question or best completes each sentence.

1. Before the end of the war, Abraham Lincoln offered a glimpse of his idea for Reconstruction through the:
   a. Wade Davis Bill.
   b. Military Reconstruction Act.
   c. Emancipation Proclamation.
   d. "Ten Percent Plan."

2. One result of the Civil War was:
   a. the recognition of the autonomy and sovereignty of the various states.
   b. the realization that the Constitution created a voluntary union of states.
   c. the growing authority that the federal government had over the states.
   d. an amendment to the Constitution that prevented future secession.

3. Andrew Johnson:
   a. was a Radical Republican who sought to remake the South in the image of the North.
   b. was a self-made man who hated the planter aristocracy.
   c. was unforgiving and used his pardon powers sparingly.
   d. followed Congress's led in pursuing Reconstruction policy.

4. Under Johnson's policy of "restoration":
   a. the South was broken into five military districts.
   b. Southern legislatures passed the racially restrictive Black Codes.
   c. large Southern landowners had their property seized and redistributed to freedmen.
   d. the Freedmen's Bureau became his favored organization for handling local problems.

5. Radical Republicans wanted to do all of the following in the South except:
   a. promote free labor.
   b. institute universal education.
   c. breakup the existing plantation system.
   d. delay civil equality for freedmen until educational reforms could take hold.

6. The Fourteenth Amendment did all of the following except:
   a. confer American citizenship.
   b. repudiate the Confederate debt.
   c. guarantee social equality.
   d. punish former Confederates.

7. In the election of 1868:
   a. Ulysses S. Grant won more than 70% of the popular vote.
   b. Ulysses S. Grant won the electoral vote but lost the popular vote.
   c. African American males enjoyed universal voting rights in the North and the South.
   d. African Americans in the South voted overwhelmingly for the Republican Party.

8. The impeachment proceedings against Andrew Johnson:
   a. ended with him being removed from office.
   b. allowed Democrats to regain the presidency in 1868.
   c. set a precedent that presidents would not be removed for political disagreements.
   d. were a resounding victory for President Johnson and ended Congressional Reconstruction.

9. During Reconstruction African Americans:
   a. tested the ability to move about freely.
   b. sought to be reunited with family members separated during slavery.
   c. hoped to acquire land.
   d. all of the above.

10. The "crop lien" system:
    a. compelled most southerners to plant cotton, which undermined the economic vitality of the region.
    b. provided an effective means of restoring economic growth to the war-devastated areas of the South.
    c. proved devastating to African-American southerners but had little real influence on white farmers.
    d. created a network of state banks that were encouraged to provide low-interest loans to farmers.

11. In the northern United States during the 1870s:
    a. factory production expanded to create the world's largest manufacturing economy.
    b. the high demand for corn led to a remarkable growth of the agricultural sector.
    c. the massive immigration of former slaves forced up wages and lowered profits.
    d. for the first time the number of wage earners surpassed the number of farmers.

12. By 1877 the Democrats:
    a. were no longer a viable party in the South.
    b. had regained political control in all of the former Confederate states.
    c. abandoned white supremacy as a political stance in the South.
    d. successfully convinced most African Americans to abandon the Republican Party.

13. In the 1870s the Republican Party:
    a. suffered because of economic problems and scandals within the party.
    b. continued to dominate national politics as it had during the Civil War.
    c. lost influence in the South but had no real opposition in the North.
    d. lost the support of the American people and failed to win any elections.

14. White Southerners who joined the Republican Party:
    a. were derisively known as scalawags.
    b. were often Whigs before the war.
    c. were often Unionists during the war.
    d. all of the above.
    e. b & c only

15. Which of the following was not a reason Reconstruction came to an end in the South:
    a. a national recession in the 1870s eroded the public's will to continue reform in the South.

b. Republicans failed to establish a permanent Republican majority in most Southern states.
c. Northern Democrats were able to regain the House of Representatives.
d. President Ulysses S. Grant lost faith in the effort in 1877.

Thought Questions: Think carefully about the following questions or comments. Your answers should prepare you to participate in class discussions or help you to write an effective essay. In both class discussions and essays you should always support the arguments you make by referring to specific examples and historical evidence. You may use the space provided to sketch out ideas or outline your response.

1. Describe the differences between presidential and congressional reconstruction. When and why were these differing policies pursued? How much of the Radical vision was implemented in either of these programs of Reconstruction?

2. Discuss the implications of Reconstruction for former slaves. How did southern African Americans manifest their freedom following the Civil War? In what ways did Reconstruction succeed or fail to deliver all that it had hoped to gain?

3. Discuss how Reconstruction influenced the lives of white Southerners.

4. How did economic considerations in the 1870s replace the South as the nation's number one problem? What were the major challenges facing capital and labor at this time?

Map Skills: These questions are based on the maps in the chapter. Please use the blank map provided here for your answers.

1. Locate the five military districts established during Reconstruction. Identify the areas that had the highest concentration of sharecroppers in 1880.

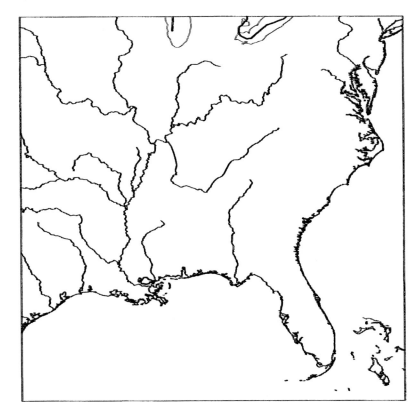

2. Indicate which states voted for Rutherford B. Hayes and which states voted for Samuel J. Tilden. Which states submitted contested returns?

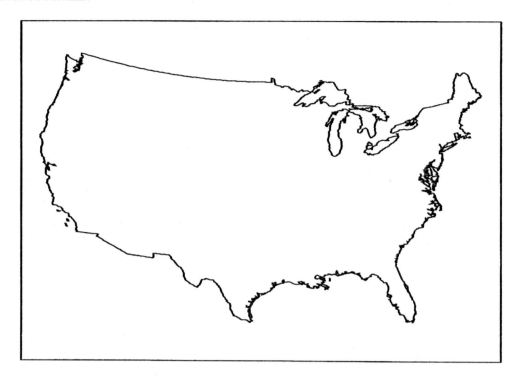

Interpreting the Past

Name _____ Date _____

Discuss the living conditions of freed blacks in the Reconstruction Era South.

DOCUMENT 1

Source: "Address from the Colored Citizens of Norfolk, Virginia, to the People of the United States" (1865)

We believe our present position is by no means so well understood among the loyal masses of the country, otherwise there would be no delay in granting us the express relief which the nature of the case demands. It must not be forgotten that it is the general assumption, in the South, that the effects of the immortal Emancipation Proclamation of President Lincoln go no further than the emancipation of the Negroes then in slavery, and that it is only constructively even, that that Proclamation can be said, in any legal sense, to have abolished slavery, and even the late constitutional amendment, if duly ratified, can go no further; neither touch, nor can touch, the slave codes of the various southern States, and the laws respecting free people of color consequent therefrom, which, having been passed before the act of secession, are presumed to have lost none of their vitality, but exist, as a convenient engine for our oppression, until repealed by special acts of the State legislature. By these laws, in many of the southern States, it is still a crime for colored men to learn or be taught to read, and their children are doomed to ignorance; there is no provision for insuring the legality of our marriages; we have no right to hold real estate; the public streets and the exercise of our ordinary occupations are forbidden us unless we can produce passes from our employers, or licenses from certain officials; in some States the whole free Negro population is legally liable to exile from the place of its birth, for no crime but that of color; we have no means of legally making or enforcing contracts of any description; we have no right to testify before the courts in any case in which a white man is one of the parties to the suit, we are taxed without representation, and, in short, so far as legal safeguards of our rights are concerned, we are defenceless before our enemies. While this is our position as regards our legal status, before the State laws, we are still more unfortunately situated as regards our late masters. The people of the North, owing to the greater interest excited by war, have heard little or nothing, for the past four years, of the blasphemous and horrible theories formerly propounded for the defence and glorification of human slavery, in the press, the pulpit and legislatures of the southern States; but, though they may have forgotten them, let them be assured that these doctrines have by no means faded from the minds of the people of the South; they cling to these delusions still, and only hug them closer for their recent defeat. Worse than all, they have returned to their homes, with all their old pride and contempt for the Negro transformed into bitter hate for the new-made freeman, who aspires for the suppression of their rebellion.

DOCUMENT 2

Source: Carl Schurz, Report on the Condition of the South (1865)

In which direction will these people be most apt to turn their eyes? Leaving the prejudice of race out of the question, from early youth they have been acquainted with but one system of labor, and with that one system they have been in the habit of identifying all their interests. They know of no way to help themselves but the one they are accustomed to. Another system of labor is presented to them, which, however, owing to circumstances which they do not appreciate, appears at first in an unpromising light. To try it they consider an experiment which they cannot afford to make while their wants are urgent. They have not reasoned calmly enough to convince themselves that the trial must be made. It is, indeed, not wonderful that, under such circumstances, they should study, not how to introduce and develop free labor, but how to avoid its introduction, and how to return as much and as quickly as possible to something like the old order of things. Nor is it wonderful that such studies should find an expression in their attempts at legislation. But the circumstance that this tendency is natural does not render it less dangerous and objectionable. The practical question presents itself: Is the immediate restoration of the late rebel States to absolute self-control so necessary that it must be done even at the risk of endangering one of the great results of the war, and of bringing on in those States insurrection or anarchy, or would it not be better to postpone that restoration until such dangers are passed? If, as long as the change from slavery to free labor is known to the southern people only by its destructive results, these people must be expected to throw obstacles in its way, would it not seem necessary that the movement of social "reconstruction" be kept in the right channel by the hand of the power which originated the change, until that change can have disclosed some of its beneficial effects?

DOCUMENT 3

Source: Clinton B. Fisk, Plain Counsels for Freedmen (1865)

I come to speak to you this evening about work; yes, work, good, honest, hard work. Do not turn away, and say you will not hear me,-that you know all about it, and that it is not a good subject for a lecture.

Listen! The very first verse of the Holy Bible tells us that God is a worker,-that in six days he made all this great world on which we dwell, and the sun and moon and stars.

All the holy angels in heaven are very busy. They go forth to do the will of the Great Being, and find their greatest bliss in action.

Good and great men are all hard workers. And do you know what it is that makes a free state so rich and strong? It is, above all things save God's blessing, patient, honest work.

There is nothing degrading in free labor,-nay, it is most honorable. Why, when God placed Adam and Eve in the garden of Eden, before either of them had ever done any wrong thing, and while they were as pure as the angels, he made gardeners of them. He required them to dress the garden and keep it nice and in good condition.

The blessed Saviour himself worked at the bench, at the carpenter's trade, until he was about thirty years of age.

And yet, some very silly people are above work,-are ashamed to have hard hands,-and do their best to get through the world without honest toil.

But this was not the case with Abraham Lincoln, the man who wrote the Proclamation of Emancipation. He used the hoe, the ax, and the maul, cleared ground, and fenced it with the rails he had split, and was ready to turn his hands to any honest work.

I know that it is quite natural that you should associate work with slavery, and freedom with idleness, because you have seen slaves working all their lives, and free people doing little or nothing. And I should not blame you if you should ask, "What have we gained by freedom, if we are to work, work, work!"

Now, let me explain. A slave works all his life for others. A free man works for himself,-that is, he gets pay for his labor; and if he saves what he earns and manages well, he can get on so well that he may spend the afternoon of his life in his own pleasant home, and never want for any thing. . .

DOCUMENT 4

Source: Mississippi Black Code (1865)

Sec. 6. Be it further enacted, That all contracts for labor made with freedmen, free Negroes, and mulattoes for a longer period than one month shall be in writing and in duplicate, attested and read to said freedman, free Negro, or mulatto, by a beat, city or county officers, or two disinterested white persons of the country in which the labor is to be performed, of which each party shall have one; and said contracts shall be taken and held as entire contracts, and if the laborer shall quit the service of the employer, before expiration of his term of service, without good cause, he shall forfeit his wages for that year, up to the time of quitting.

DOCUMENT 5

The Memphis Riot (1866)
Source: The Freedmen's Bureau Online, Records of the Assistant Commissioner for the State of Tennessee,
Bureau of Refugees, Freedmen, and Abandoned Lands, 1865–1869. National Archives Microfilm Publication
M999, roll 34 "Reports of Outrages, Riots and Murders, Jan. 15, 1866–Aug. 12, 1868."
http://www.freedmensbureau.com/tennessee/outrages/memphisriot.htm

Report of an investigation of the cause, origin, and results of the late riots in the city of Memphis made by Col.
Charles F. Johnson, Inspector General States of Ky. and Tennessee and Major T. W. Gilbreth, A. D. C. to Maj.
Genl. Howard, Commissioner Bureau R. F. & A. Lands.

The remote cause of the riot as it appears to us is a bitterness of feeling which has always existed between the low
whites & blacks, both of whom have long advanced rival claims for superiority, both being as degraded as human
beings can possibly be.

In addition to this general feeling of hostility there was an especial hatred among the city police for the Colored
Soldiers, who were stationed here for a long time and had recently been discharged from the service of the U.S.,
which was most cordially reciprocated by the soldiers.

This has frequently resulted in minor affrays not considered worthy of notice by the authorities. These causes
combined produced a state of feeling between whites and blacks, which would require only the slightest
provocation to bring about an open rupture...

Action of Bvt. Brig. Genl. Ben P. Runkle, Chief Supt., Bureau R.F. and A.L. Sub-District of Memphis

General Runkle was waited upon every hour in the day during the riot, by colored men who begged of him
protection for themselves and families, and he, an officer of the Army detailed as Agent of the Freedmen's Bureau
was suffered the humiliation of acknowledging his utter inability to protect them in any respect. His personal
appearance at the scenes of the riot had no affect on the mob, and he had no troops at his disposal...

The origin and results of the riot may be summed up briefly as follows:

The remote cause was the feeling of bitterness which as always existed between the two classes. The minor
affrays which occurred daily, especially between the police and colored persons.

The general tone of certain city papers which in articles that have appeared almost daily, have councilled the low
whites to open hostilities with the blacks.

The immediate cause was the collision heretofore spoken of between a few policemen and Negroes on the evening
of the 30th of April in which both parties may be equally culpable, followed on the evening of the 1st May by
another collision of a more serious nature and subsequently by an indiscriminate attack upon inoffensive colored
men and women.

Three Negro churches were burned, also eight (8) school houses, five (5) of which belonged to the United States
Government, and about fifty (50) private dwellings, owned, occupied or inhabited by freedmen as homes, and in
which they had all their personal property, scanty though it be, yet valuable to them and in many instances
containing the hard earnings of months of labor.

DOCUMENT 6

Source: The Fourteenth Amendment (1868)

Sec. 1. All persons born or naturalized in the United States, and subject to the jurisdiction thereof, are citizens of
the United States and of the State wherein they reside. No State shall make or enforce any law which shall abridge
the privileges or immunities of citizens of the United States; nor shall any State deprive any person of life, liberty,
or property, without due process of law; nor deny to any person within its jurisdiction the equal protection of the
laws.

Sec. 2. Representatives shall be apportioned among the several States according to their respective numbers, counting the whole number of persons in each State, excluding Indians not taxed. But when the right to vote at any election for the choice of electors for President and Vice President of the United States, Representatives in Congress, the Executive and Judicial officers of a State, or the members of the Legislature thereof, is denied to any of the male inhabitants of such State, being twenty-one years of age, and citizens of the United States, or in any way abridged, except for participation in rebellion, or other crime, the basis of representation therein shall be reduced in the proportion which the number of such male citizens shall bear to the whole number of male citizens twenty-one years of age in such State.

Sec. 3. No person shall be a Senator or Representative in Congress, or elector of President and Vice President, or hold any office, civil or military, under the United States, or under any State, who, having previously taken an oath, as a member of Congress, or as an officer of the United States, or as a member of any State legislature, or as an executive or judicial officer of any State, to support the Constitution of the United States, shall have engaged in insurrection or rebellion against the same, or given aid or comfort to the enemies thereof. But Congress may by a vote of two-thirds of each House, remove such disability.

Sec. 4. The validity of the public debt of the United States, authorized by law, including debts incurred for payment of pensions and bounties for services in suppressing insurrection or rebellion, shall not be questioned. But neither the United States nor any State shall assume or pay any debt or obligation incurred in aid of insurrection or rebellion against the united States, or any claim for the loss or emancipation of any slave; but all such debts, obligations and claims shall be held illegal and void.

Sec. 5. The Congress shall have power to enforce, by appropriate legislation, the provisions of this article.

DOCUMENT 7

Source: James T. Rapier, Testimony Before U.S. Senate Regarding the Agricultural Labor Force in the South (1880)

A. Well, sir, there are several reasons why the colored people desire to emigrate from Alabama; one among them is the poverty of the South. On a large part of it a man cannot make a decent living. Another is their want of school privileges in the State: and there is a majority of the people who believe that they cannot any longer get justice in the courts; and another and the greatest reason is found in the local laws that we have, and which are very oppressive to that class of people in the black belt.

Q. State what some of them are.

A. First, we have only schools about three months in the year, and I suppose I need not say anything more on that head. In reference to the poverty of the soil, 33 to 40 per cent of the lands in Alabama is about all on which a man can make a living.

Q. Do you mean the parts that are subdued?

A. Yes, sir; the arable land. The average is one-third of a bale of cotton to the acre, not making three bales to the hand; and a hundred bushels of corn to the hand, on an average. Then take the price of cotton for the last two years; it has not netted more than $45 to $47.50 to the bale; and I suppose it would not be amiss for me to state something of the plans of working the land in Alabama.

Mr. Vance. It will be very proper.

The Witness. The general plan is that the landlord furnishes the land and the teams and feed for the teams and the implements, for which he draws one half of the crop. I remarked that the three bales of cotton and a hundred bushels of corn is about all that you can make to a hand. We allow in Alabama that much, for that is as much as a man can get out of it, and that is not enough to support his family, including himself and the feed of his family; $95 to $100 is as much as a hand can make, and that is not enough to feed any man in a Christian country. . . .

DOCUMENT 8

Source: A Sharecrop Contract (1882)

To every one applying to rent land upon shares, the following conditions must be read, and agreed to.

To every 30 and 35 acres, I agree to furnish the team, plow, and farming implements, except cotton planters, and I do not agree to furnish a cart to every cropper. The croppers are to have half of the cotton, corn, and fodder (and peas and pumpkins and potatoes if any are planted) if the following conditions are complied with, but-if not-they are to have only two-fifths (2/5). Croppers are to have no part or interest in the cotton seed raised from the crop planted and worked by them. No vine crops of any description, that is, no watermelons, muskmelons, . . . squashes or anything of that kind, except peas and pumpkins, and potatoes, are to be planted in the cotton or corn. All must work under my direction. All plantation work to be done by the croppers. My part of the crop to be housed by them, and the fodder and oats to be hauled and put in the house. All the cotton must be topped about 1st August. If any cropper fails from any cause to save all the fodder from his crop, I am to have enough fodder to make it equal to one-half of the whole if the whole amount of fodder had been saved…

I am to gin & pack all the cotton and charge every cropper an eighteenth of his part, the cropper to furnish his part of the bagging, ties, & twine. The sale of every cropper's part of the cotton to be made by me when and where I choose to sell, and after deducting all they owe me and all sums that I may be responsible for on their accounts, to pay them their half of the net proceeds. Work of every description, particularly the work on fences and ditches, to be done to my satisfaction, and must be done over until I am satisfied that it is done as it should be.

Answer Key

Chapter One

SHORT RESPONSE: 1. Chahokia 2. Indios 3. Asia 4. Clovis 5. 15,000 6. Corn Mother 7. forest efficiency 8. Maya 9. Great Plains 10. Iroquois Confederacy

MULTIPLE CHOICE ANSWERS: 1-B (p. xlviii); 2-B (p. 3); 3-C (p. 5); 4-B (pp. 3-4); 5-D (pp. 5-8); 6-D (pp. 9-11); 7-C (p. 11); 8-A (p. 11); 9-A (p. 10); 10-B (pp. 11–12); 11-A (p. 13); 12-C (pp. 14-15); 13-B (pp. 16-20); 14-A (p. 20); 15-B (p. 18)

Chapter Two

SHORT RESPONSE 1. Virginia Dare 2. Sir Walter Raleigh 3. Feudalism 4. Renaissance 5. Vasco da Gama 6. encomienda 7. Bartolome de Las Casas 8. Ponce de Leon 9. Treaty of Tordesillas 10. Martin Luther

MULTIPLE CHOICE ANSWERS: 1-B (p. 24); 2-D(p. 27); 3-D (pp. 28-29); 4-B (pp. 29-30); 5-C (p. 30); 6-D (p. 30); 7-A (pp. 30-31); 8-D (p. 31); 9-A (p. 32); 10-C (p. 36); 11-B (pp. 33-34); 12-D (p. 42); 13-C (p. 39); 14-B (p. 44); 15-C (p. 40)

Chapter Three

SHORT RESPONSE: 1. Santa Fe 2. exclusion 3. Mestizos 4. engages 5. New Amsterdam 6. Powhatan 7. Opechancanough 8. Mayflower 9. William Bradford 10. Anne Hutchinson

MULTIPLE CHOICE ANSWERS: 1-D (pp. 48-49); 2-A (pp. 50-51); 3-B (pp. 52–53); 4-A (p. 54); 5-D (p. 55); 6-B (p. 58); 7-C (p. 58); 8-C (p. 60); 9-D (p. 61); 10-A (pp. 54-65); 11-B (p. 64); 12-D (p. 68); 13-A (p. 70); 14-A (p. 71); 15-C (p. 66)

Chapter Four

SHORT RESPONSE: 1. Stono Rebellion 2. Royal Africa Company 3. Rhode Island 4. Middle Passage 5. Virginia 6. Chesapeake 7. Elizabeth Lucas Pinckney 8. Florida 9. John Woolman's 10. Great Awakening

MULTIPLE CHOICE ANSWERS: 1-C (p. 74); 2-C (p. 76); 3-A (p. 78); 4-B (p. 78); 5-D (pp. 78-79); 6-A (pp. 82-83); 7-C (p. 86); 8-D (p. 86); 9-C (pp. 87-88); 10-A (p. 90); 11-B (p. 90); 12-D (pp. 93-95); 13-C (p. 95); 14-C (pp. 99-100); 15-B (pp. 100-101)

Chapter Five

SHORT RESPONSE: 1. Jonathan Edwards 2. Great Awakening 3. Spanish Borderlands 4. French Crescent 5. John Locke 6. Pennsylvania 7. Backcountry 8. Middling Sort 9. Robert Walpole 10. democracy

MULTIPLE CHOICE ANSWERS: 1-C (p. 104); 2-D (p. 108); 3-C (p. 110); 4-A (p. 112); 5-B (p. 114); 6-C (p. 115); 7-C (pp. 116-118); 8-A (p. 118); 9-B (p. 110); 10-C (pp. 120-121); 11-B (p. 123); 12-D (p. 127); 13-A (p. 126); 14-A (p. 125); 15-C (p. 130)

Chapter Six

SHORT RESPONSE: 1. Philadelphia 2. Patrick Henry 3. Albany Conference 4. Cajuns 5. Treaty of Paris 6. Royal Proclamation 7. "Cato's Letters" 8. James Otis 9. Sugar Act 10. Boston

MULTIPLE CHOICE ANSWERS: 1-B (p. 134); 2-D (p. 137); 3-D (p. 138); 4-B (pp. 138-140); 5-C (p. 142); 6-B (p. 141); 7-B (p. 144); 8-A (p. 148); 9-B (pp. 149-150); 10-C (pp. 146-147); 11-C (p. 152); 12-A (p. 151); 13-D (p. 153); 14-D (p. 158); 15-C (pp. 156-159)

Chapter Seven

SHORT RESPONSE: 1. Valley Forge 2. Continental Army 3. Loyalists or Tories 4. Benedict Arnold 5. Mercy Otis Warren 6. Delaware River 7. Saratoga 8. Yorktown 9. John Trumbull 10. Articles of Confederation

MULTIPLE CHOICE ANSWERS: 1-A (p. 168); 2-D (p. 169); 3-C (p. 169); 4-B (p. 172); 5-A (p. 174); 6-B (p. 176); 7-A (p. 177); 8-B (p. 177); 9-D (p. 179); 10-D (p. 180); 11-A (p. 183); 12-C (p. 187); 13-A (p. 188); 14-B (pp. 188-189); 15-D (pp. 189-190)

Chapter Eight

SHORT RESPONSE: 1. Shays' Rebellion 2. Philadelphia 3. Virginia Plan 4. slave, slaves or slavery 5. Anti-Federalists 6. Federalists 7.The Federalist Papers 8. Rhode Island 9. Bill of Rights 10. Whiskey Rebellion

MULTIPLE CHOICE ANSWERS: 1-B (p. 194); 2-C (p. 195); 3-C (p. 197); 4-D (p. 197); 5-B (pp. 198-199); 6-B (pp. 203-204); 7-C (p. 202); 8-C (p. 204); 9-A (p. 205); 10-C (p. 210); 11-B (p. 212); 12-A (p. 213); 13-B (p. 212); 14-B (p. 211); 15-B (p. 213)

Chapter Nine

SHORT RESPONSE: 1. Sacajawea 2. Columbia 3. Philadelphia 4. Russians 5. Haiti 6. Kentucky, Tennessee 7. cotton gin 8. Virginia dynasty 9. Thomas Malthus 10. Chief Justice John Marshall

MULTIPLE CHOICE ANSWERS: 1-D (p. 221); 2-B (p. 224); 3-B (p. 224); 4-B (p. 226); 5-C (p. 228); 6-A (p. 227); 7-D (p. 226); 8-C (pp. 226-227); 9-B (p. 229); 10-D (p. 235); 11-A (p. 239); 12-B (p. 231); 13-A (p. 233); 14-A (p. 245); 15-C (p. 245)

Chapter Ten

SHORT RESPONSE: 1. James Henry Hammond 2. Hinton Rowan Helper 3. cotton 4. 60%, $200 million 5. internal slave trade 6. 1808 7. 75% 8. The Great Awakening 9. Nat Turner 10. yeoman

MULTIPLE CHOICE ANSWERS: 1-C (p. 250); 2-C (p. 253); 3-A (p. 255); 4-C (p. 255); 5-B (p. 255); 6-A (p. 256); 7-D (p. 262); 8-B (p. 258); 9-A (p. 266); 10-B (p. 268); 11-C (p. 261); 12-D (p. 264); 13-B (pp. 266-267); 14-A (pp. 272-273); 15-C (p. 273)

Chapter Eleven

SHORT RESPONSE: 1. Working Men's Party 2. Andrew Jackson 3. 90% 4. property owners or taxpayers 5. "corrupt bargain" 6. Martin Van Buren 7. "Age of the Common Man." 8. Peggy Eaton 9. Henry Clay 10. nullification

MULTIPLE CHOICE ANSWERS: 1-C (p. 298); 2-C (p. 280); 3-C (p. 281); 4-D (p. 284); 5-D (pp. 284-285); 6-A (p. 287); 7-B (p. 288); 8-D (p. 291); 9-B (p. 291); 10-D (p. 292); 11-B (p. 294); 12-C (p. 295); 13-D (p. 298); 14-B (p. 297); 15-A (p. 297)

Chapter Twelve

SHORT RESPONSE: 1. Lowell, Massachusetts 2. National Road 3. Erie Canal 4. Robert Fulton 5. Baltimore and Ohio 6. Market Revolution 7. putting out system 8. John Deere 9. Samuel Slater 10. American System of Manufactures

MULTIPLE CHOICE ANSWERS: 1-B (p. 308); 2-D (p. 308); 3-A (p. 310); 4-D (p. 312); 5-D (p. 310); 6-B (p. 312); 7-A (p. 316); 8-B (p. 316); 9-D (p. 317); 10-A (p. 326); 11-C (pp. 322-323); 12-D (pp. 323-325); 13-C (p. 327); 14-A (p. 328); 15-C (p. 331)

Chapter Thirteen

SHORT RESPONSE: 1. Declaration of Sentiments 2.Elizabeth Cady Stanton 3. Antislavery or Temperance 4. New York City 5. New Orleans 6. 48% 7. Potato Famine 8. California Gold Rush 9. epidemics 10. perfectionism

MULTIPLE CHOICE ANSWERS: 1-B (p. 334); 2-B (p. 337); 3-D (p. 338); 4-A (p. 341); 5-A (p. 338); 6-A (p. 345); 7-A (pp. 338-341); 8-C (pp. 341-343); 9-A (p. 350); 10-C (p. 352); 11-B (p. 349); 12-D (p. 349); 13-C (p. 350); 14-A (p. 355); 15-B (pp. 355-357)

Chapter Fourteen

SHORT RESPONSE: 1. Juan Nepomuceno Seguín 2. General Antonio López de Santa Anna 3. Lewis and Clark 4. Great American Desert 5. Oklahoma 6. Frederick Jackson Turner 7. John O' Sullivan 8. Donner Party 9. Fifty-Four Forty or Fight!! 10. Santa Fé Trail

MULTIPLE CHOICE ANSWERS: 1-C (p. 362); 2-A (p. 365); 3-D (p. 369); 4-B (p. 372); 5-D (pp. 365-374); 6-C (p. 369); 7-C (pp. 369-370); 8-C (p. 377); 9-D (pp. 379-380); 10-A (p. 377); 11-B (pp. 379-377); 12-A (p. 384); 13-D (p. 385); 14-D (p. 380); 15-B (pp. 382-383)

Chapter Fifteen

SHORT RESPONSE: 1. Stephen Douglas, Abraham Lincoln 2. Uncle Tom's Cabin 3. John C. Calhoun 4. Slave Power 5. gag rule 6. wage slavery 7. popular sovereignty 8. personal liberty laws 9. Anthony Burns 10. Ostend Manifesto

MULTIPLE CHOICE ANSWERS: 1-A (p. 392); 2-B (p. 396); 3-C (p. 396); 4-A (p. 399); 5-D (p. 398); 6-C (p. 402); 7-B (p. 401); 8-C (p. 404); 9-A (p. 406); 10-B (p. 409); 11-B (p. 403); 12-D (p. 411); 13-B (p. 411); 14-C (p. 412); 15-C (p. 413)

Chapter Sixteen

SHORT RESPONSE: 1. Mary Ann Bickerdyke 2. Fort Sumter 3. Baltimore 4. 620,000 5. Jefferson Davis 6. Legal Tender Act 7. cotton diplomacy 8. Confederacy 9. George B. McClellan 10. Vicksburg

MULTIPLE CHOICE ANSWERS: 1-D (p. 424); 2-D (p. 424); 3-D (p. 425); 4-C (p. 425); 5-A (p. 427); 6-D (p. 428); 7-C (p. 429); 8-D (p. 434); 9-C (pp. 434-435); 10-D (pp. 435-436); 11-B (p. 438); 12-A (p. 437); 13-C (p. 442); 14-B (p. 443); 15-A (p. 444)

Chapter Seventeen

SHORT RESPONSE: 1. Union League 2. Ku Klux Klan 3. Fourteenth Amendment 4. Ku Klux Klan Act 5. forty acres and a mule 6. Andrew Johnson 7. Black Codes 8. Tenure of Office 9. Fifteenth Amendment 10. tenant farming, sharecropping

MULTIPLE CHOICE ANSWERS: 1-D (p. 452); 2-C (p. 451); 3-B (p. 453); 4-B (p. 453); 5-D (p. 454); 6-C (p. 455); 7-D (p. 457); 8-C (pp. 455-456); 9-D (pp. 458-461); 10-A (p. 471); 11-D (p. 472); 12-B (p. 477); 13-A (p. 474); 14-D (p. 466); 15-D (pp. 475-477)